PUBLIC POLICY IN CHINA

Recent Titles in
Contributions in Political Science

Principled Diplomacy: Security and Rights in U.S. Foreign Policy
Cathal J. Nolan

Presidential Influence and Environmental Policy
Robert A. Shanley

Professional Developments in Policy Studies
Stuart Nagel

County Governments in an Era of Change
David R. Berman, editor

First World Interest Groups: A Comparative Perspective
Clive S. Thomas

Cold War Patriot and Statesman: Richard M. Nixon
Leon Friedman and William F. Levantrosser, editors

Legislators, Law and Public Policy: Political Change in Mississippi and the South
Mary DeLorse Coleman

Provisional Irish Republicans: An Oral and Interpretive History
Robert W. White

The Political World of a Small Town: A Mirror Image of American Politics
Nelson Wikstrom

Ownership, Control, and the Future of Housing Policy
R. Allen Hays, editor

The Presidency in an Age of Limits
Michael A. Genovese

Leftward Ho! V. F. Calverton and American Radicalism
Philip Abbott

Public Administration in China
Miriam K. Mills and Stuart S. Nagel, editors

PUBLIC POLICY IN
——CHINA——

EDITED BY

Stuart S. Nagel & Miriam K. Mills

Prepared under the auspices of the
Policy Studies Organization

CONTRIBUTIONS IN POLITICAL SCIENCE
NUMBER 318

Greenwood Press
WESTPORT, CONNECTICUT • LONDON

Library of Congress Cataloging-in-Publication Data

Public policy in China / edited by Stuart S. Nagel and Miriam K. Mills;
prepared under the auspices of the Policy Studies Organization.
    p.   cm. — (Contributions in political science, ISSN 0147–1066
no. 318)
    Includes bibliographical references and index.
    ISBN 0–313–28848–8 (alk. paper)
    1. China—Social policy. I. Nagel, Stuart S.
II. Mills, Miriam K. III. Policy Studies Organization. IV. Series.
HN733.5.P83   1993
361.6′1′0951—dc20   92–37519

British Library Cataloguing in Publication Data is available.

Library of Congress Catalog Card Number: 93–37519
ISBN: 0–313–28848–8
ISSN: 0147–1066

First published in 1993

Greenwood Press, 88 Post Road West, Westport, CT 06881
An imprint of Greenwood Publishing Group, Inc.

Printed in the United States of America

The paper used in this book complies with the
Permanent Paper Standard issued by the National
Information Standards Organization (Z39.48–1984).

10 9 8 7 6 5 4 3 2 1

Dedicated to improving public policy
in the People's Republic of China
and to the memory of Miriam Mills
and the students of Tiananmen Square
who worked toward achieving that goal.

Contents

Tables and Figures

TABLES

Preface: Chinese Policy Studies

Public policy studies can be defined as the study of the nature, causes, and effects of alternative ways by which governments deal with social problems. The most interesting aspects of policy studies relate to evaluating the effects of alternatives, although knowing the nature and causes of the alternatives is important to understanding why some policies are adopted more readily than others.

Evaluating alternative public policies in a systematic way involves processing a set of societal goals to be achieved, policy alternatives available for achieving the goals, and relations between goals and alternatives in order to arrive at or explain the best alternative, combination, allocation, or predictive decision-rule. That concept of policy studies is geographically independent, since it applies across countries. It is also independent of subject matters, since it is applicable to economic, social, technological, political, or legal policy problems.

PREMODERN DEVELOPMENTS

In some ways China has been well ahead of the rest of the world in the development of policy studies but behind in other ways. When much of the Western world was in the process of converting from warlike Teutonic tribes into nation-states, China had a well-developed and -studied governmental system. One could find insights into governmental decision making in the writings of Confucius and others before Aristotle, Machiavelli, and other Western governmental scholars began to write.

However, when the Western world was undergoing its revolutions, such as those in France and the Untied States, China was still associated with authoritarian dynastic government. When the Western world was undergoing industrial change and social reform through relatively peaceful means associated with the New Deal and western European socialist parties, China and the Soviet Union were undergoing revolutionary ideological change.

IDEOLOGY, TECHNOCRACY, AND SYNTHESIS

In the 1970s, the People's Republic of China (PRC) was seeking to resolve public policy problems largely by consulting the ideological writings of Karl Marx, Mao Zedong, and their interpreters. In the 1980s, government agencies in China were seeking to become more professional by introducing personnel management, financial administration, and other bureaucratic ideas from the West, some of which are actually a throwback to Confucius bureaucracy.

Thus, ideology became offset by technocracy. What we were seeing may fit the classic Hegelian and Marxist dialectic of thesis, antithesis, and synthesis. Ideology represented the prevailing thesis in the 1970s, whereby population control might be analyzed by reading Marx and Mao. Technocracy represented the antithesis in the 1980s, whereby population control might be analyzed by reading biological literature.

The 1990s may represent a super-optimum synthesis (SOS) of the best, not the worst, of both possible worlds. It may draw on the idea of having goal-oriented values from the ideological thesis, as contrasted to rejecting values as being unscientific or not objective. Values and goals may be quite objective in the sense of being provable means to higher goals or in the sense of proving that certain alternatives are more capable of achieving the goals than others.

The 1990s may also draw on the idea of empirical proof based on observable consequences, rather than ideological labels of socialism or capitalism. It is empirical proof that also makes sense in terms of deductive consistency with what else is known about the world, rather than mindless technical number crunching without thinking about how the results might fit common sense. Being technical does not necessarily mean being effective in getting the job done efficiently and equitably, which is what should really count in governmental decision making.

MOVING TO A SUPER-OPTIMUM SYNTHESIS (SOS)

The kind of synthesis to which SOS refers is a synthesis of goals to be achieved (the ideological element) and systematic methods for determining which alternative or alternatives most achieve these goals (the technical element). The true dialectic is dynamic not only in the sense that a thesis leads to an antithesis, which leads to a higher-level synthesis, but also in the sense that a synthesis does not stagnate but becomes a subsequent thesis to be resynthesized by a new antithesis into a still higher level of analysis. There may be policy evaluation methods that are even more effective, efficient, and equitable.

Those are the methods that are hinted at in various places in this book where super-optimum solutions are explicitly or implicitly mentioned. Such solutions enable conservatives, liberals, and other viewpoints to all come out ahead of their best initial expectations simultaneously. Traditional optimizing involves finding the best alternative or alternatives in a set. SOS analysis involves finding an alternative that is better than what conservatives previously considered the best and simultaneously better than what liberals previously considered the best, using both conservative and liberal values.

ALTERNATIVES, GOALS, AND RELATIONS AS SUPER-OPTIMIZING INPUTS

Table 1, "Super-Optimizing Analysis Applied to the Chinese Excess Population Problem," can be used to illustrate what is meant by super-optimizing policy analysis where all major viewpoints can come out ahead of their best initial expectations. The title uses the words *excess population* rather than *population problem* because most of China's so-called population problem does not relate to a surplus of people but rather to a shortage of production. Some of the population problem (at least in the short run) may, however, relate to a strain on China's current resources, a strain that can be lessened by lessening the number of consumers.

The alternatives are listed in the vertical column. The conservative alternative (which is the most regulatory) is to try to enforce a strict one-child policy. The liberal alternative (which allows the most freedom) is to be completely flexible on family size. This alternative is also possibly the most similar to Marxist ideology, which tends to view population control as a capitalistic idea designed to either increase the population of the poor (in order to have a reserve army of unemployed people) or to decrease the population of the poor (out of fear that the poor will overwhelm the middle class). These two Marxist views tend to nullify each other, possibly leading one to the conclusion that there is no Marxist view on population policy. The compromise position between conservative regulation and liberal freedom is to have a one-child policy with various exceptions, such as allowing a second child if the first is a daughter or allowing a second child among rural but not urban people.

The first key goal is small families, given the tremendous burden on the Chinese economy and government services of a billion people reproducing at a rate greater than one child per family. Even one child per family would mean substantial short-run population growth because people are living longer. If one simplifies the arithmetic by saying that if the 500 million males marry the 500 million females and have one child per couple within the next few years, then the population would grow from one billion to 1.5 billion. The increase of 500 million is more people than every country of the world currently has with the exceptions of China and India. The rich may not get richer, but the highly populated get even more highly populated.

The second key goal is reproductive freedom. Even the conservatives recognize the interfering with reproductive freedom makes for a lot of antagonism toward

Table 1
Super-Optimizing Analysis Applied to the Chinese Excess Population Problems

CRITERIA / ALTERNATIVES	C Goal Small Families	L Goal Reproduc-tive Free-dom	N Total (Neutral Weights)	L Total (Liberal Weights)	C Total (Conservative Weights)
C Alternative Strict One-Child Policy	4	2	12	10	14*
L Alternative Flexible on Family Size	2	4	12	14*	10
N Alternative One Child With Exceptions Allowed	3	3	12	12	12
S Alternative Remove Causes of Excess Children	5	5	20	20**	20**

NOTES:

1. Relevant causes of excess children in the China population context include:
   (1) The need for adult children to care for their elderly parents which could be better handled through social security and/or jobs for the elderly.
   (2) The need for extra children to allow for child mortality, which could be better handled through better child health care.
   (3) The need for male children in view of their greater value, which could be better handled through providing more opportunities for females.
   (4) The lack of concern for the cost of sending children to college which could be better handled through a more vigorous program of recruiting rural children to college.
2. It is not a super-optimum solution to provide monetary rewards and penalties in this context because:
   (1) The monetary rewards for having fewer children enable a family to then have more children.
   (2) The monetary punishments for having more children stimulate a family to have still more children to provide offsetting income.
   (3) The monetary rewards and punishments are made meaningless by the simultaneous policies which are increasing prosperity in rural China.

   * Conservative or liberal winner without considering the SOS.
  ** Conservative or liberal winner when SOS is considered.

the government. Thus, both goals are endorsed by both conservatives and liberals, but Chinese conservatives place relatively more emphasis on small families and Chinese liberals place relatively more emphasis on reproductive freedom.

The relations between the alternatives and the goals provide a classic trade-off. A strict one-child policy is good for small families but bad for reproductive freedom. Flexibility on family size is good for reproductive freedom but bad for small families. The effect of the compromise alternative is mediocre on both. This compromise is better than the worst for both small families and reproductive freedom, but it is clearly not better than the best expectations for either goal.

SUBSIDIES AND CAUSES

In many public policy problems, the super-optimum solution involves well-placed subsidies and tax breaks, but well-placed tax breaks are meaningless in a Communist society. Under communism, people do not do much direct tax paying (especially income taxes), as they do in Western societies. Instead, the government is supported by paying people less than they are worth in their government jobs. The difference is a hidden tax. Ironically, this fits well the Marxist idea of surplus-value exploitation of labor. It is an easy form of tax to collect, but it does not allow for the use of tax breaks as incentives.

China has tried subsidizing small families by giving monetary rewards to those who have small families and monetary punishments to those who do not. The effect has been almost the opposite of the government's intent. The subsidies to small families have in many instances increased the families' income so they can now afford to have more children. Having a monetary punishment or reduced salary may even motivate parents to have an additional child to help bring in more income to offset the reduced salary. Also, moving simultaneously toward a more prosperous free market (especially in farm products) has enabled many rural people now to have more children and not be bothered by the withdrawal of subsidies or other monetary punishments.

A kind of super-optimum solution may make more sense for dealing with the Chinese population problem. It could provide small families and reproductive freedom simultaneously. Doing so requires looking to the causes of having additional children and then trying to remove or lessen those causes. One cause is a need to have children who will support parents in their old age. Adopting a more effective social security system helps eliminate or lessen that cause.

Another cause is having additional children as backup because the death rate is high among rural Chinese children under age five. Various forms of pediatric public health, such as giving shots and using effective remedies to prevent life-jeopardizing infant diarrhea and dehydration, can make a big difference.

A third cause is the widespread feeling that female children are worthless and do not bring honor to the family. Families therefore keep trying until at least one son is born. That cause can be substantially lessened by the new moves in China toward much greater opportunities for women to become lawyers and doctors and to enter other prestigious occupations. In China, women's liberation has facilitated birth control, whereas in the United States birth control has done more to facilitate women's liberation.

REFERENCES AND OTHER EXAMPLES

For further details on public policy analysis of China's population problems, see Judith Banister, *China's Changing Population* (Stanford University Press, 1987), and Jean Robinson, "Of Family Policies in China," in Richard Hula and Elaine Anderson, eds., *The Family and Public Policy* (Greenwood Press, 1991).

I first systematically generated the super-optimizing ideas while lecturing at People's University of China in Beijing in May–June 1989. They arose from such examples as providing special food stamps to keep food prices low to urban consumers while keeping food prices high to rural farmers but with strings attached to stimulate urban and rural productivity in return for the food stamps. Another example was providing salary increases to professors through a system of low tuition and scholarships while keeping down government expenses and the burden on the taxpayer. Examples like these are discussed in various places in this book, but especially in Part 3.

ORGANIZATION OF THE BOOK

The chapters that follow are organized into four parts: (Part I) background on public policy in China, including policy studies by Tang Daiwang and political science by Zhao Baoxu; (Part II) specific policy problems, including social security by Peter Lee; health care by Sun Guangde; environmental protection by Hon S. Chan, K. C. Cheung and Jack M. K. Lo; and economic development by Thomas R. Dye; (Part III) policy analysis methods, including super-optimizing analysis and Chinese policy problems by Stuart S. Nagel and SOS analysis applied mainly to Hong Kong problems by King W. Chow; and (Part IV) diverse overall evaluations from the insider's perspective of Xia Shuzhang and from the frequent visitor's perspective of King W. Chow.

ACKNOWLEDGMENTS

Many people have been helpful in the development of this book. Most of them were involved in making possible the itinerary of scholarly interactions in China from May 21 through June 7, 1989. They include the following: L. Z. Yuan of the Asia Foundation and John Kim of the Midwest University Consortium for International Affairs, who provided funding for the trip; King W. Chow of the Political Science Department at the University of Hong Kong, who served as an expert translator, adviser, and friend throughout the trip; people from universities in Hong Kong, such as Benjamin Ostrov, Lo Chen Sik-Sze, and N. J. Miners; people from government agencies in Hong Kong, such as Leo Goodstadt, R. J. Hoare,

Linus Cheung, Chan Wing-Kwai, Stephen Chung, and Daniel Sreepny; people from Zhongshan (Sun Yat-Sen) University in Guangzhou (Canton), such as Xia Shuzhang, Guo Weiqing, Le Fu Wang, and Liu Yuelun; people from the Institute of Cadres Training and South China University in Guangdong Province, such as Tang Daiwang, Li Huajie, Shen Zhao Wu, and Cal Hannan; people from the National School of Administration and the People's University of China in Beijing, such as Huang Da-qiang, Li Kangtai, Zhao Lu-Kuan, and Jao Jian; people from Beijing University, such as Zhao Baoxu, Zhang Ying-qing, Xie Qingkui, Liang Shou-de, Wenxiang Gong, Shi Zhifu, and Fang Lianqing; people from the Chinese Public Administration Society, such as Liu Yichang and Guo Bing-yu; people from the Ministry of Machinery and Electronics Industry, such as Shi Lichuan, Wu Wenfeng, Fu Weimin, Miao Qipei, Zhang Bing-Chang, Liang Shihe, Peng Jian, and Ma Fhigiang; people from the Beijing municipal and district governments, such as Duan Bingren, Shen Ren-Dou, and Wang Ji Ping; Ambassador James Lilley and the American embassy personnel; and those who are involved in translating into Chinese this book and other related policy analysis books, such as Han Chun-Li, Zhang Jinma, Shao Yong Wu, and Zhou Chao. Thanks are also owed to Mildred Vasan and Marcia Goldstein for their helpful editing of this and other Greenwood books and to numerous people in the streets, campuses, and government offices of Hong Kong, Guangzhou, and Beijing whose names were not obtained but who were helpful in offering their opinions of matters relevant to public administration and public policy in the People's Republic of China.

PART I

Background on Public Policy in China

CHAPTER 1

Policy Studies in China

Tang Daiwang

Tang Daiwang considers the development of policy studies within the People's Republic of China. There has been considerable attention to the problems of public policy in dealing with social issues; even Mao Zedong spoke of the importance of determining the proper policy for management interaction and relationships. With the goal of unifying society, one had to determine methods for dealing with internal conflicts.

In considering the relevant characteristics of policy analysis, the author points to the special regard for this field shown by Chinese rulers. The intelligentsia has also been strongly involved. One of the difficulties in establishing policies is to be responsive to problem resolution but still remain in line with the central authority.

Policy analysis is enormously important for the People's Republic of China, but Tang suggests that the techniques and research still require further construction and modification. It was only in 1985 that policy analysis began to be studied as a scientific discipline. The goal of educators is to establish policy science, building on relevant practices from other parts of the world but staying consistent with and responsive to the Chinese experience.

Within China, socialism was constructed on a foundation that was partially colonial and partially feudal. Those origins, rather than a capitalistic basis, have led to complexity in the establishment of a systematic policy science. The huge population and uneven economic development have also led to difficulty. The author points out that some of the greatest problems have come about from ignoring economic and developmental principles, as exemplified in the great leap forward and the cultural revolution.

Rational and careful analysis of the field will require effort. Given the enormous changes now occurring within the People's Republic of China, social development calls for the interaction of policy science. Steadily, policy studies institutes, which specialize in the teaching of this new field, are being established. An example is Tang's own institution, Guangdon, Institute of Administration.

Where civil servants are being trained and research is developing, there is a need for usable policy sciences, as well as the development of a substructure of research and education to sustain those efforts. The author notes the importance of utilizing what is worthwhile from the international policy science field but also of building on what is appropriate and responsive to the Chinese perspective.

The development of Chinese public administration (PA) as a field of study in the past few years has been impressively rapid. Nevertheless, policy studies (PS), which may be considered a critical component of PA, has yet to receive similar attention and support. This chapter will give an account of its development and issues; the objective is to promote a better understanding of Chinese PS among scholars, within and outside China, so that more concerted efforts will be directed to the development of Chinese PS.

One note deserving elaboration is that the arguments to be presented in the following sections are based on, first, my interactions (in the past three decades) with 1,000-plus state cadres (civil servants), including many who were involved in policy analysis works, and second, my interactions with 100-plus PA scholars, as well as analysis of current PA curricula, course contents, and PA texts.

DEVELOPMENT OF POLICY STUDIES IN CHINA

Public policy scholars in America, as compared with traditional public administrators and public management scholars, are latecomers. PS (or policy analysis) as an area of professional study has become popular only after eight universities launched, in the early 1970s, their policy studies programs: Berkeley Graduate School of Public Policy, the Carnegie-Mellon School of Urban and Public Affairs, Duke's Institute of Policy Sciences, Public Affairs, Harvard's John F. Kennedy School of Government, the Michigan Institute of Public Policy Studies, Stanford's Public Management Program within its Graduate School of Business, Texas's Lyndon B. Johnson School of Public Affairs, and the RAND Graduate Institute (Ellwood 1985, 18–19).

Policy Studies as a Field

This is also the case in China. After Professor S. Z. Xia (1982) called for a systematic study of administration, public administration as an academic discipline became a legitimate field of study. Many universities and cadre-training institutes have established PA programs or offer PA courses while hundreds of scholars consider it their specialty. Yet, very few PA scholars have underscored the significance of PS or have strived to have it established.

At the moment, there is one major school of thought that stresses decision making and considers it the core of PA study. Scholars subscribing to this school of thought are mainly those who have received training in economics and quantitative analysis. They advocate the systematic study of decision-making models and techniques. Their concerns for the improvement of decision making are reflected in all current PA curricula: students are required to take at least one course, usually labeled "Administrative Decision Making." Since the leadership has repeatedly called for the improvement of efficiency and effectiveness in state organs, and thus has placed a premium on rational decision making, these scholars are well received in both the academic community and government offices and are heavily influencing the perception of PA students toward the dynamic nature and characteristics of decision making in public organizations.

One important point about the current wisdom of this school of thought is that although scholars have not employed the concept of policy analysis, they have set the distinction between "administrative decision making at the state level" and "administrative decision making in state organs": the former carries the characteristics of policy analysis as described in American PA literature; the latter refers to the daily problem-solving activities.

Based on interactions with PA scholars at various official functions, such as the annual conference of the Association of PA Teaching and Research, I believe that close to 100 PA scholars are decision-making scholars (there are now approximately 1,000 scholars claiming PA as their specialty). Moreover, my analysis of current PA curricula and course contents indicates that the overwhelming majority of decision-making scholars are concerned with administrative decision making in state organs.

If we are in agreement with Dwight Waldo (Brown and Stillman 1985) that PA scholars should forget about the definitional problem and just treat PA as an *enterprise*, a term broad enough to cover all the activities pursued by scholars and practitioners, we may then label decision-making scholars as PS scholars. But this general treatment is undesirable. In the United States, the focus of public policy programs is not administrative decision making. Policy analysis is the business of U.S. programs; the thrust of their core curricula is to build policy analysis skills (Ellwood 1985, 42).

Moreover, the pedagogical goal of those policy programs is to provide three educational experiences: (1) the mastery of a body of largely quantitative skills derived from the disciplines of economics, operations research, statistics, and applied mathematics; (2) the experience of the workshops and electives, to allow the student to apply these skills to several policy problems; and (3) an exposure to political and organizational analysis (Ellwood 1985, 50). In this light, it is obvious that PS is much more than administrative decision-making analysis.

Furthermore, "policy analysis is not the subject matter for a course, but rather is the business of the entire program . . . and that business is very different from the content of the policy analysis courses found in most political science oriented graduate programs for the public service" (Ellwood 1985, 42). For many political scientists, policy analysis is a subfield of their discipline that seeks to explain why a given policy came about. "It is what Duncan MacRae has labeled 'explanatory analysis.' This approach is process-oriented, descriptive rather than instrumental, and relatively qualitative rather than quantitative" (Ellwood 1985, 41).

To public policy scholars, the concern is creating an interdisciplinary common body of knowledge that can be used by analysts in an instrumental way. In doing so, they have moved away from the descriptive approach of political science and have built a curriculum around systematic analysis and optimization techniques found in economics, applied mathematics, and operations research. In adopting an interdisciplinary approach, they have rejected the politics-administration dichotomy; their aim is to aid the choice of the correct policy rather than to administer whatever policy the political process produces (see Ellwood 1985 for a more detailed account of the scope, nature, and characteristic of PS).

In China, a handful of PS scholars holds a similar viewpoint and strive to accomplish similar goals. Specifically, these scholars choose to focus on public policy as the unit of analysis. They are also concerned with both the analysis *of* and *in* policy-making; that is, they try to do descriptive studies to account for the causes and effects of various public policies and aim to conduct analytic studies for the improvement of both the policy-making process and policy analysis tools and techniques. Thus, they are vitally concerned with such issues as meaningful transfer of analytic skills and techniques from Western democracies to socialist China, systematic comparison among policy alternatives, effective program evaluation, and necessary formulation and reformulation of metapolicy. Since 1985, some Chinese PA scholars have translated journal articles and books on foreign policy studies. Their objective is to introduce to Chinese scholars and practitioners the development, as well as the scope and nature, of PS in Western democracies.

Unfortunately, the goals and struggles are too much for the PS scholars. This has to be the case because the development of PS as a field of study is still at the early stage. The rapid development of Chinese PA in the 1980s was possible because there were scholars, such as Professor S. Z. Xia, who had received graduate training in PA from American universities in the 1940s; based on the PA knowledge learned in America, they could at least offer PA courses and write books, even though some of their understanding may be erroneous or outdated. In comparison, PS is a latecomer in the United States, and thus none of the first generation of Chinese PA scholars had the opportunity to systematically learn about the feature, theories, methodology, and issues of PS. Thus, there are no leading scholars to push for a rapid development. PS scholars lack the training, inspiration, and leadership to more rapidly achieve the pedagogical and practical goals of PS.

At the moment, there are approximately twenty PA scholars who consider PS their specialty or offer PS courses; that is, less than 2 percent of scholars are PS scholars. More than ten young Chinese scholars are now in the United States pursuing graduate training in PS; their eventual return to China would substantially contribute to the development of the field. As of today, however, the strength is very limited; so too is the contribution by the PS scholars.

It should be noted that some researchers may consider the number of Chinese PS scholars to be much bigger than I have suggested. Obviously, if we include all those researchers who have an interest in the study of a particular substantive policy, such as education, health care, population control, and environmental protection, the number of PS scholars may be substantially increased. Yet, these scholars, who work at either universities and colleges or research institutes (established specifically for the purpose of promoting research on a particular policy), are primarily concerned with "analysis of policy making," that is, with accounting for the causes and effects of a particular policy and with giving policy recommendations. They have little interest in developing PS as a field. For example, researchers pursuing studies on environmental protection are not concerned with whether environmental protection as a regulatory type of policy is more difficult to get adopted (and to implement) as compared with education, which is a distributive type of policy. In other words, they have little interest in addressing such theoretically important questions as whether or not the nature of different policies would affect the levels of politicization of policy-making and implementation. As such, their contribution to the development of PS as a science is limited, although their research findings may serve as a basis for formulating policy analysis theories. In this light, these scholars should not be labeled PS scholars; the terms "peripheral PS scholars" is more appropriate.

Policy Studies as a Professional Activity

Whereas Chinese PS as a field of study is a new invention, the practice of policy analysis is not. Specifically, PS as a professional pursuit has been well established in China since the 1930s. When the Chinese Communists established their revolutionary basis in Yanan, their leaders pushed for systematic analysis of policies and programs. Cadres were often sent to various localities to collect information about the economic, social, and political problems, such as education, agricultural development, and health care. Those cadres were required to submit reports that described the problems and presented remedial-action plans.

After 1949, the leadership further stressed the significance of systematic policy analysis and instructed all state organs (whether ministries under the State Council, bureaus of provincial governments, or the central office of prefectural/county governments) to formally establish a policy study office (PSO), called "Policy Analysis Office" (*Zhengce yanjiushi*) or "Investigation Analysis Office" (*Diaocha yanjiushi*). Members of PSO were administrative cadres responsible for collecting and analyzing data about some pressing policy problems and for giving piecemeal advise or presenting complete policy/program plans for action. Whereas the team of PS scholars is small, the number of practitioners is not. Hard data is unavailable, but a reasonable estimate of the total number of PSO staff is 30,000-plus: the typical establishment of PSO is 10 cadres, and there are more than 2,000 county government and 1,000-plus central and provincial state organs. Thus, close to .7 percent of all cadres (4 million-plus) are involved in policy analysis work.

Moreover, advice and action plans presented by PSO are often well received. Based on my interactions with PSO staff at the levels of county, provinces, and State Council ministries I have learned that in the 1950s PSO played a very significant role in the policy formation stage: policymakers usually rejected policy proposals that were not endorsed by PSO; many policy proposals adopted were those initiated by PSO, whereas others were adopted only after modifications as recommended by PSO. After the fall of the "Gang of Four," PSO again resumed its important role. It is true that not all advice or proposed action plans presented by PSO would be adopted. Yet, almost all (present or past) leading cadres (officials in charge) at all levels had worked in PSO. This informal staffing practice reflects the genuine significance of PSO.

In addition to the increasing PSO influence is the recent stress on policy analysis and program evaluation. Since the late 1970s, the leadership has been vitally concerned with rational decision making. Thus, many of the policy analysis rules and procedures that were stipulated in the 1950s have been reinstated. For example, it was a typical practice that leading cadres of a particular ministry, province, or prefect would meet at least twice a year to consider possible policy reformulation. During the meetings, they would discuss the changing characteristics of a policy problem, the effectiveness of the programs being implemented, and the necessary adjustments to be made. Since the late 1970s, these biannual meetings, the so-called Five Level Winter-Spring Meetings (*Wuji dongchun dahuui*), are again mandated: state organs at the levels of State Council ministry, province, municipality, county, and town (village) must hold two meetings in late spring and early winter, respectively. Moreover, some of these meetings have been turned into teleconferences so that more cadres can participate and many leading cadres will not have to travel too far to participate.

The mandated collective effort to conduct policy analysis and program evaluation is one major measure reinstated. The other one is provision of systematic training in policy analysis. Specifically, training was popular before the cultural revolution (1966–76): many cadres, particularly those well performed, were required to participate in short-term training programs; program participants were to study political theories, policy principles of socialist China, and examples of effective policy-making and program implementation; program instructors were university teachers and leading cadres. These programs were abolished during the cultural revolution. Since 1984, many cadres have been selected to attend PA training programs offered by cadre-training institutes at the provincial level or the State Council ministry level. In 1988, a bureau-grade cadre, Sun Jiao-liang, offered a course on public policy analysis—the first of its kind—at the Training Institute of the Ministry of the Machine Building Industry, in which he systematically introduced to program participants the significance of public policy analysis and the "theories" (or principles) of production, industrial development, and economic policy-making. Although he could not offer the same course again in 1989 or 1990 because of his heavy workload, his course was well received and has drawn substantial attention from both practitioners and the academic community.

Practitioners are particularly interested in rational policy analysis as described by Sun; after attending the course, they also recognize that they have yet to acquire, possibly from scholars, rigorous training in policy analysis and program evaluation.

To more systematically advance the science and art/craft of policy analysis, the National School of Administration has been working closely with the Institute of Administrative Sciences at the People's University of China to train PS researchers/teachers and to translate academic works on policy analysis and program evaluation. Some of the scholars and practitioners involved have also entertained an idea of establishing a graduate program of policy analysis. One key administrator of the National School of Administration has also contacted two leading universities in the United States to discuss the possibility of establishing joint doctoral (public administration/policy) programs. These developments all reflect the regime's active promotion of rational policy analysis.

In short, PS as a professional pursuit has been well established. Nevertheless, professional analysts have received little rigorous training in policy analysis and program evaluation, and thus they have yet to realize rational policy-making. Given the fact that the leadership has placed a premium on effective policy analysis, these analysts are in the position to contribute a more rapid development of PS. But this requires the presence of two conditions: first, scholars must strive to upgrade their ability to offer training programs for the enhancement of practitioners' professional knowledge and skills so that practitioners will appreciate the values and significance of PS and will more actively participate in the pursuit of developing the field; second, scholars and practitioners must work closely together to promote theory building and the effective transfer of knowledge. These two conditions, however, are hardly easy to enhance because there are various problems confronting scholars and practitioners.

CRITICAL ISSUES

The recent development of PS as a professional activity may be impressive, but the profession has had critical problems, as has PS as a field of study. The first is theory-building, which is also a serious problem in the United States, as Ingraham (1987) has noted:

When confronting policy problems . . . agencies turn to similar agencies, states to other states, and nations to other nations in the common search for problem solution. What is missing is a serious effort to determine the exact nature of the problem and its causes, the potential range of solutions, and the most appropriate strategy for achieving desired outcomes. Also notably absent is a theory, or sets of theories, the purpose of which is to guide policy design (p. 613).

The Problem of Theory-Building

In the case of China, due to the inadequate training in theory-building, Chinese researchers are not well prepared to conduct "analysis in policy-making," the search for improvement of metapolicy, metatheory, and methodology that are essential to the formulation, as well as implementation, of specific substantive policies. They can merely translate foreign publications or write descriptive reports, and they have nothing theoretical to offer to practitioners.

Seemingly, Chinese PS scholars are following the steps of American scholars. In the United States, there is a consensus that "policy studies should be systematic, relevant to the needs of decision makers, and cross-disciplinary" (Hedge and Mok 1987, 50). Nevertheless, as Hedge and Mok (1987) have noted, a content analysis of 300 articles published between 1975 and 1984 in six major policy journals reveals that policy research "often falls short of what has essentially become the textbook view of policy studies (i.e., systematic, relevant, and multidisciplinary)" (Hedge and Mok 1987, 57). Other scholars have also been critical. "The emerging discipline of public policy studies is characterized by a growing disjunction between theory and research. While there are many provocative and potentially important theories, systematic empirical research to test them has largely been lacking" (Greenberg, Miller, Mohr, and Vladeck 1977, 1532). In sum, as Haveman (1987) concludes, "Much of what passes as policy analysis and evaluation research does not meet . . . the standard of social science disciplines" (209).

American scholars' theory-building performance may be unsatisfactory, but this should not be an excuse for Chinese PS scholars. Fortunately, many Chinese scholars do recognize that their performance is unsatisfactory and that they are still in the stage of marketing—advocating the significance of policy analysis and calling for the advancement of PS as a science and an art. More important, they realize that without theories they are hardly in the position to legitimize the field and to influence policy-making in the government.

Peripheral PS scholars, who are primarily concerned in specific substantive policies, have also failed to contribute. Because of their training, they are merely interested in "analysis of policy-making"—trying to account for the causes and effects of a particular policy and to give policy recommendations. Since they pay little attention to the "analysis of policy-making," their contribution to the improvement of both the policy-making process and policy analysis tools has been very limited. Moreover, since most Chinese social scientists are hardly well trained in social scientific investigation, they have tended to conduct merely descriptive studies. As such, their research on the making of specific substantive policies has yielded relatively little systematic knowledge that can serve as a basis for formulating or testing theoretical propositions about that particular policy.

Professional policy analysts—the 30,000-plus cadres—are not doing any better. Although they have been systematically collecting and analyzing data, they, just like the peripheral PS scholars, have been pursuing "analysis of policy-making." Specifically, they have been doing "goal-based empirical policy research," which searches for ways to cope with specific policy problems. Since their policy problems are idiosyncratic, their research findings cannot be generalized. Besides, these practitioners have neither the interest nor the training to do generalization. As such, their research works have contributed little to theory-building. Thus, they have no "theories" for guiding the making of metapolicy or substantive policies. In addition, due to various political movements launched in the past decades, many of them have developed a habit of adopting some "principles" or "world views" and treating them as "theories." For example, in the 1950s and 1960s some believed that imperialism was the cause of all problems and that socialism was the panacea for all problems; in the early 1980s, some believed, "Who cares about principles as long as it works?" They thus have not felt the need to conduct "analysis in policy-making."

Socialist China is a developing country with more than one billion in population. Its economic, social, and political problems are inevitably complex and difficult to handle. Thus, there is a need to conduct not only "analysis of" policy-making but "analysis in" as well. The latter is paramount if policy theories are to be established. Yet, professional analysts and PS scholars, core or peripheral, have not been able to give much contribution. This is mainly because they have yet to receive rigorous training in positive research, the second serious problem to be discussed in this chapter.

Inadequate Training in Positive Research

To account systematically for the causes and effects of various public policies and to improve both the policy-making process and the policy analysis tools and techniques, PS should become a social science basing on positive research. In the United States, however, there has been a heated debate among scholars about the role and contribution of positive research.

Specifically, social scientific research has sought to understand the world of human and social behavior. Moreover, "the process of social research involves model building, hypothesis formulation and testing, and in general the application of the scientific method" (Haveman 1987, 192). Most American policy analysts in the 1960s and 1970s subscribed to the notion of positivism: they believed in the critical role played by social scientific research methods in the pursuit of modifying public policies: their emphasis was on the application of scientific method, statistical models, and research designs. But in the 1980s, many researchers have criticized this subscription. For example, Kelly (1986) argues:

policy inquiry cannot be unobtrusive. By measuring we intrude on reality and, therefore, change it. We cannot separate ourselves from the phenomena being studied. . . . We interact with it, and because humans are involved, reality is willfully reshaped. The resulting variations in our units of analysis made generalizations unreliable and invalid . . . policy inquiry based on the logic and methods of traditional applied social science of such changeable entities, such moving targets, is not realistic, not empirical, and not useful for improving public sector performance. (526)

Guba (1985) also notes:

Policy analysis is essentially a value-based enterprise. Whether or not a policy of ameliorating the conditions of the poor is a good or useful policy depends on value-judgements, not scientific data. Policy analysis's closest cousin is what [is] commonly called a *needs-assessment*. Despite the pretensions of many needs assessors that it is a purely scientific process, it is also heavily value based. (12)

The critic goes on:

Policy analyses cannot be conducted reasonably within the limits posed by the positivist inquiry paradigm. A value based entity cannot be effectively explored through a putatively value free epistemology. Scientific defensibility cannot be permitted to supersede the many moral, ethical, and pragmatic criteria that a society, especially a pluralistic society, has a right to expect in policy determinations. And in all events, the notion that policies can fruitfully be conceived as causes whose effects can be validly assessed should be repudiated. (Guba 1985, 15)

In short, many contemporary American scholars are suspicious. They generally believe that "policy analysis is viewed as involving values, politics, emotion, and subjectivity and the attempt to overlay the assumptions of positivist science is seen as misguided" (Bozeman 1986, 519).

In China, the situation is different. Although policy analysis would inevitably involve subjectivity and may not be purely "positive," Chinese PS scholars have yet to acquire adequate training in positive research so that they could be in a better position to decide on what research methods to be employed to examine what policy problems with what precautions to take. More important, almost all Chinese PS scholars are not prepared for conducting systematic and objective study of policy problems. They often fail, based on factual information collected, to establish typology for further analysis; they invariably fail to establish generalizations that are reliable and valid, since they are unaware of the differences between empirical propositions and normative principles; they often look at policy issues from a narrow perspective that is framed by their personal experiences and needs.

In the United States, PS scholars may have relied too much on positive research, which cannot account fully for the dynamics of policy-making politics. In China, the problem is an insufficient application of scientific methodology. Moreover, although many American PS scholars may not have conducted policy studies that are systematic, relevant, and multidisciplinary, they at least have received rigorous training to do so. In China, this is not the case: Chinese scholars are unable to apply such simple methods as before-and-after comparison to evaluate program effectiveness; many are unfamiliar with stakeholders analysis, which is essential to the formulation and implementation of politically feasible programs; others are unable to use even oval diagrams to identify the many causes and effects of a policy problem, never mind about computer applications and statistical analysis; still others are unaware of the difficulties of comparative analysis and of the pitfalls of case study.

In short, due to inadequate training in positive research, Chinese PS scholars are hardly in the position to conduct systematic, logical, objective, and empirically rigorous research. They are merely capable of doing idiosyncratic descriptive studies that contribute little to even the "analysis of policy-making." Positive research, as current critics in the United States have reflected, is not the only way to generate usable knowledge. But Chinese PS scholars need the training so that they will not be forever conducting nonpositive research that cannot result in the formulation of the empirically verified propositions that are essential to the advancement of knowledge about humanity and to the resolution of practical problems.

Politics, Policy, and Values

The third problem confronting Chinese PS scholars revolves around politics and values. Policy analysis may involve such nonhuman elements as mechanical forces, but policy formulation must inevitably involve human values and emotion. As McAdams (1984) has rightly pointed out, "The benefits of health, education, and welfare programs are diverse and often intangible." In addition, "No amount of analysis is going to tell us whether the Nation benefited more from sending a slum child to pre-school, providing medical care to an old man or enabling a disabled housewife to assume her normal activities." After all, "The 'grand decisions'—how much health, how much education, how much welfare, and which groups in the population shall benefit—are questions of value judgements and politics." Thus, "policy analysts cannot make much contribution to their resolution" (95).

To ensure effective contribution to policy-making, PS scholars must be vitally concerned with values. This includes policymakers' values. Thus, as Bozeman (1986) argues:

For maximum impact the findings of policy analysis must be incorporated in the working knowledge . . . of public decision-makers. Even assuming that policy scientists have properly read and responded to the *logic* of decision-making, it is increasingly clear that policy analysis is not sufficiently attentive to the *psychology* of decision-making. The conceptual frameworks and cognitive styles which policy-makers bring to decision processes determined the usefulness of analytically-based policy analysis. (527, emphasis in original)

In China, this is a fundamental problem with which PS scholars find it difficult to cope. Specifically, the Chinese policy-making process is highly politicized. Various leaders, due to their personal values, committed goals, and past experiences, employ various political strategies and tactics to have their preferred policies adopted and implemented. Because of one key feature of Marxist-Leninist state structure—centralism—leaders may do many things not found in Western democracies or even in the history of China, such as launching the cultural revolution. Thus, there has been an absence of striking regularities of policy-making behavior. Moreover, since access to information is limited, there has been a lack of basis for PS scholars to evaluate policymakers' values and their relation to the formulation of particular policies. In light of these constraints, the findings of Chinese policy analysis can hardly be incorporated in the working knowledge of policymakers. Thus, those findings have a very limited effect on policy-makers.

But this is only one aspect of the problem; the other side is that the findings of Chinese policy analysis have not been incorporated in the working knowledge of the masses, who in theory can participate in policy making. Specifically, Chinese PS scholars, including the peripheral scholars, have often overlooked the conceptual frameworks and cognitive styles that the masses bring to the decision-making process. They have yet to conduct systematic surveys or even unobstructive observations to find out what influences the masses to be responsive to what type of policy/programs under what situation and with what effects. Scholars are thus hardly in the position to conduct studies that generate politically feasible and technically sound policy proposals for resolving practical problems confronting the masses.

Such a pursuit could be fruitful. For example, birth control has been ineffective, and researchers could not come up with measures that would promote voluntary birth control. Until recently, some researchers have paid attention to the mentality of the masses and found that the general public would try to break the birth control law because many of them felt that having more children was the only effective means to ensure a financially secure life after retirement. This finding then served as a basis for reformulating the birth control policy. The government now gives money to those who have only one child, and the money is automatically deposited in a special bank account that the parents will have access to after retirement. Many people now feel secure and have voluntarily complied with the birth control law.

Unfortunately, most PS scholars, as well as practitioners, have yet to underscore the significance of assessing the values and needs of the masses. They are thus unable to establish empirical propositions about how the one billion–plus Chinese would perceive and react in various policy situations. Thus, their influence on the formulation of policies is limited.

In the United States, policy analysts are becoming more sensitive to social values, with more questioning of goals when evaluating alternative policies. As Nagel (1990) has noted:

A number of research and training programs across the country now emphasize the analysis of goals, rather than, or in addition to, the achievement of goals, such as the programs at Notre Dame, Maryland, Georgetown, Duke, Delaware, and the Hastings Institute. Goals can be analyzed through survey research to determine to what extent they are supported, relational analysis to determine how achieving them would affect higher values, or philosophical analysis to determine how they fit into more general philosophical systems. (425)

Chinese PS scholars have yet to strive for the establishment of these kinds of programs. They should.

All in all, politics and values are critical components of policy analysis that scholars must not overlook. Nevertheless, Chinese PS scholars have intentionally and unintentionally avoided them. This avoidance has adversely affected the advancement of usable policy knowledge and of knowledge of human behavior, never mind the establishment of PS programs that strive to make policy analysis compatible with the more general philosophical system in China. Seemingly, PS scholars should be vitally concerned with values and politics; they should strive for repoliticization of public administration.

CONCLUSION

The Chinese PS as a field of study is still in its early development stage. There are various issues that scholars should be vitally concerned with. Due to the political sensitivity and complexity of those issues, a comprehensive, in-depth analysis cannot be presented here. All we can conclude are that Chinese PS scholars are seemingly unprepared to more forcefully and fruitfully establish the field and that practitioners are in need of assistance from scholars. I personally believe that Chinese scholars are intelligent and trainable and that assistance from scholars in Western democracies is essential to a more rapid development of PS as a field of study and as a professional activity.

ACKNOWLEDGMENT

The author wishes to thank Dr. King W. Chow for his contribution to the preparation of this chapter. I consider him a de facto coauthor.

REFERENCES

Bozeman, Barry. 1986. "The Credibility of Policy Analysis: Between Method and Use." *Policy Studies Journal* 14(4):519–39.
Brown, Brack, and Richard J. Stillman II. 1985. "A Conversation with Dwight Waldo: An Agenda for Future Reflections." *Public Administration Review* 45(4):459–67.
Ellwood, John William. 1985. "A Morphology of Graduate Education for Public Service in the United States." Report for the Study of Trends and Innovations in Graduate Education for Public Service, by the National Association of Schools of Public Affairs and Administration.
Greenberg, George D., Jeffrey A. Miller, Lawrence B. Mohr, and Bruce C. Vladeck. 1977. "Developing Public Policy Theory: Perspectives from Empirical Research." *American Political Science Review* 71(4):1532–43.
Guba, Egon G. 1985. "What Can Happen as a Result of a Policy?" *Policy Studies Review* 5(1):11–16.
Haveman, Robert H. 1987. "Policy Analysis and Evaluation Research after Twenty Years." *Policy Studies Journal* 16(2):191–218.

Hedge, David M., and Jin W. Mok. 1987. "The Nature of Policy Studies: A Content Analysis of the Policy Journal Articles." *Policy Studies Journal* 16(1):49–62.

Ingraham, Patricia W. 1987. "Toward More Systematic Consideration of Policy Design." *Policy Studies Journal* 15(4):611–28.

Kelly, Rita M. 1986. "Trends in the Logic of Policy Inquiry: A Comparison of Approaches and a Commentary." *Policy Studies Review* 5(3):520–28.

McAdams, John. 1984. "The Anti-Policy Analysis." *Policy Studies Journal* 13(1):91–102.

Nagel, Stuart S. 1990. "Conflicting Evaluations of Policy Studies." In Naomi B. Lynn and Aaron Wildavsky, eds., *Public Administration: The State of the Discipline*. Chatham, N.J.: Chatham House Publishers.

Webber, David J. 1986. "Analyzing Political Feasibility: Political Scientists' Unique Contribution to Policy Analysis." *Policy Studies Journal* 14(4):545–53.

Xia Shuzhang. 1982. *Renmin Ribao*, January 29.

APPENDIX: POLICY STUDIES IN THE PEOPLE'S REPUBLIC OF CHINA
By Tang Daiwang and Zhou Chao

As the economy and technology of the United States developed rapidly after World War II, social problems became complicated. To help the government formulate and execute public policy and deal more effectively with social issues, some scholars in the 1950s advocated the study of policy science. The discipline began to take shape in the early 1960s and was further developed in the 1970s. By the 1980s, policy studies had become a multidisciplinary subject with strong application implications.

In China, unlike in the United States, there has been a long tradition of policy analysis dating as far back as 400 B.C.; political analysts there have accumulated a wealth of materials on a wide range of policy areas. There are many prominent characteristics of Chinese policy analysis, including:

1. Policy analysis constitutes one of the major political processes. Chinese rulers have always paid special attention to policy formulation and execution.

2. The intelligentsia's active participation in policy formulation and evaluation is notable. People even risked their lives to submit policy proposals and suggestions to the rulers.

3. Policy analysis and decisions are mainly carried out within the government and aim at solving concrete problems; in this process, "congruence with the central authority" is stressed.

4. Chinese government is highly centralized. Disputes in the processes of implementation are referred to higher authorities for resolution.

5. There is an increasing number of non-governmental advisory bodies as well as academic groups that both seek and have increasing bearing on government policy making.

6. While policy analysis in China is pragmatic in orientation, research in theory, model building, and process studies are inadequate. As a result, policy analysis tends to adopt short-term perspectives.

7. It was not until 1985 that policy analysis was studied as a scientific discipline. At present, the endeavor is still at a preliminary stage, concentrating mainly on the translation of foreign classics and the digestion and absorption of these materials. Moreover, such studies are primarily pursued only in colleges and research institutes in the coastal regions.

8. Younger and middle-aged scholars have become the vanguard for the promotion of the discipline. Attempts are being made to assess the application of foreign doctrines to local circumstances and to connect policy analysis with policy formulation and execution. Efforts are also being made to draw generalizations from experience and to establish gradually a policy science with Chinese characteristics.

After more than forty years under socialism, Chinese people have come to realize that without policy science there will be no scientific policies. Thus, in recent years, emphasis has been put on policy science study with the aim of elevating policy making as a mere routine activity of government to a signpost of scientific governance. The prominence given to policy studies by both scholars and the government is closely related to socioeconomic and political changes.

1. For example, policy science is needed to resolve increasingly complex social problems. Socialism in China was built not on the basis of a capitalist system; rather, the transformation took place on the foundations of a semi-colonial, semi-feudal society. The restructuring of the social order and the government led to rapid and significant changes in political, economic, and cultural life. The vast population and uneven economic development among different regions further complicated the situation. While the New China government gained some initial achievements in various areas, there were also some mistakes. The Great Leap Forward went against economic principles, the cultural revolution went against developmental principles, and large-scale deforestation went against the natural order. These all resulted in massive losses of lives and resources. Pressured by the population and having learned their lessons, authorities came to realize the futility of unrealistic plans and aimless projects and to see the importance of democratic and scientific processes of policy making.

2. A relaxed political atmosphere has contributed to the emphasis on policy science. In the late 1970s, the open door policy became the national policy of China. The central government decided that to attain economic development, more use had to be made of "policy" and "science." This effectively gave a pass for the study of policy science, which used to be confined to governmental organizations. The discipline became a scientific arena for the pursuit of truth. Following the liberalization in ideology and rejuvenation of respect for the intellectual, the intelligentsia, seeing the needs of the reform programs, tried to bring in social science disciplines from the West. A vast number of classic books and theses in philosophy, economics, management science, operation research, decision science, politics science, administrative science, sociology, and psychology were translated into Chinese and gained speedy development. This lay the foundation and framework for the development of policy science in China.

3. Social development requires the guidance of policy science. China is in a historical transitional period. Both the social and economic systems are undergoing rapid transformation. Experience teaches that to realize the target of rapid social and economic development, thorough political and economic reforms have to be carried out. More systematic policies are required in various fields—the economy, finance, investment, taxation, technology, wage policies, and welfare policies—so as to maintain macro-control of the problems of inflation and inequitable allocation. Moreover, the international scene is changing rapidly. Peace and development have become the main themes of the present age. China, accordingly, has to formulate its foreign policies to accommodate such changes and to promote international communication and cooperation so as to assist the construction of its socialist modernization. Thus, both domestically and internationally, there are problems that await policy resolution; public policy analysis is an instrument for such purposes.

Due to these reasons, a new era has begun for policy analysis in China. Many policy studies institutes with multidisciplinary orientations have been established in China, such as the Economic and Technological Development Research Centre under the State Council, ranging from central to local and district levels. These agencies work at various administrative levels and concentrate on practical policy problems that cover diverse areas. Not only do they study a wide range of issues, but, at the moment, they also employ most of the personnel in the field. In some colleges and academic research units, there are also some related policy analysis agencies serving teaching and research purposes. These concern themselves mainly with the development of theory and methodology in public policy analysis. Apart from these, some big corporations and companies have also begun to recognize the relations between public policy and corporate development. They, in response, establish their own research institutes like the Social Development Strategy Research Centre of the Stone Corporation. Their main task is to study the principal policies of the government and then formulate the development strategy of their company. The establishment of these policy research institutes attracts a large number of middle-aged and young scholars. This activates and strengthens the study of policy analysis in China, promoting the development of the discipline.

In order to raise the standard of policy formulation and execution in China, the quality of the policymaker has to be improved. In recent years, various schools for administrative cadres have been established, from the central authority to local provinces and cities, specializing in training cadres from different professions and levels. Their prime objective is to improve the cadres' theoretical and educational level, especially in policy science. Some institutes even specialize in teaching policy science; the Guangdong Institute of Administration, for example, regularly invites local and foreign experts like Stuart S. Nagel to lecture and give seminars on public policy analysis. At present, hundreds of institutes of administration have been established, and tens of thousands of cadres are trained annually. The establishment of these cadre training centers and training programs provide a strong impetus for the progress of research in policy science in China.

In order to build up the theory and methodology for policy research that will suit the nation's situations, scholars have begun to systematically assemble the rich historical inheritance in policy analysis from the past, particularly the analyses and criticisms of major policy issues after 1949, studying their causes and effects and learning from those experiences. At the same time, attention is being paid to the description, prediction, explanation, and evaluation of current policies. Scholars are also actively introducing overseas research findings for learning and reference. Books and theses of the discipline, such as Robert M. Krorne's *Systems Analysis and Policy Science* and Charles E. Lindblom's *The Policy-making Process*, have been translated into Chinese. Stuart S. Nagel's *Policy Studies: Integration and Evaluation* will also be published soon. In addition, some local schools have also published their own scholars' works, such as Sun Xiaoliang's *Introduction to Policy Analysis* (Zheung Ce Yan Jia Gai Lun). This book attempts to illuminate organizational problems and the policy-making process and evaluation in China. However, there is a bulk of theoretical questions that have not yet been addressed, such as the impact of political conditions on policy decisions, the principles for policy planning, the factors affecting policy execution, and the types of policy evaluation. These all await further studies and exploration.

Policy science in China has only just begun and is still in the infancy stage. The general standard has yet to be improved, and the analysis of policy has yet to be developed into the study of policy science—that is, it has yet to advocate policies and to describe, analyze, and explain the theoretical basis, coverage, and methodology of the policy outcome. Policy science should emphasize applications that in turn will help the development of the subject. As such, five relationships have to be acknowledged and managed: cooperative relations among the policy scientist, the policy maker, and the administration; specialization and coordination among policy science, politics, and administration; relations between the promotion of national culture and absorption of western science; relations between law and policy; and relations between policy science and the power of interference.

In China, the strengthening and improvement of policy-making systems and a policy center to facilitate the flow of information, consultation, implementation, supervision, and evaluation are required. The strengthening of an effective policy evaluation system is of prime importance. This includes policy-making assessment, implementation, evaluation, impact assessment, economic efficiency analysis, and prediction assessment. Active and conscious evaluation of present policies is vital for avoiding serious mistakes in policy formulation and implementation. Evaluation is one of the functions in the policy process that communicates policy impacts to the policy-making unit. It aims at reflecting deviations in execution from the original policy objective in order to help the decisionmaker to determine whether to carry on with the existing policy or to make amendments. An assessment mechanism with various information channels and communication instruments is central for balanced policy making and implementation.

Because every nation possesses different organizational arrangements, and because their activities and characteristics also differ, there is no one best model. We have to learn from developments in policy science overseas, and we have to draw lessons from our own past experiences in policy making, especially since 1949; at the same time have to actively promote academic interflow, study policy formulation in depth, and assess the relations between theory and practice to establish policy science with Chinese characteristics.

CHAPTER 2

Political Science in China

Zhao Baoxu

Zhao Baoxu analyzes and assesses the development and current status of the political science field within contemporary China. The initial view in 1949 was to follow the example of the Soviet Union. Since there were no counterparts of political science in the Russian universities, the field of political science was abolished in 1952. It was not until 1978 that the field was resumed.

The Chinese Association of Political Science (CAPS) was established in 1932, but it was not until 1978 that it reemerged. The inaugural meeting in 1980 drew over 150 scholars from twenty-four provinces. Some of the decisions made included commitment to Marxism-Leninism as the source of guidance for the study of political science, as well as attention to creative research. Topics of interest included system reform, legislation, and relationships between the state and the political party. Interest was also expressed in learning from foreign training and experience. Currently, political science is offered at more than ten major Chinese universities, and increasingly more textbooks on political science have been published.

Subscribing to the view that "social practice is the only measure of truth," China has become steadily engaged in using productive and creative research studies to assist the government. As Professor Zhao notes, it is only within a suitable political environment that creative and bold scientific studies can be developed.

Professor Zhao points out some significant achievements since the reinstitution of the field, including a reinterpretation of class and class structure. In addition, there has been concern for the analysis of the state. He notes that scholars no longer look to the state as a tool for class repression and, instead, concentrate more on the administrative functions.

Other considerations include political power as the basis of the analysis of political science, as well as investigation of how a nation is transformed from traditional to modern standing. He speaks to greater efforts for achieving research and describes a major project in which eleven universities throughout the country assembled information on the present political system and desirable reforms. There is great movement within the field, and this is ably and insightfully described by Professor Zhao.

It is well known that since ancient times China has been characterized by a heritage rich in the study of political science. As the country with the longest history and the largest population in the world, China has accumulated rich experiences in political theory and practice as well as in administration. Most of these experiences and theories have been well preserved through the ages in written form. There is no doubt that some are out of date, but many, even today, are still valued as treasures of wisdom.

Modern Western political science was first introduced into China in the late nineteenth century. Around 1900, China published the first book of Western political science, by the Commercial Press. This book was a Chinese version of a lecture record from a German professor. The first university to offer the course of political science was the Capital Academy, today's Peking University. After the October Revolution, Marxist-Leninist theories concerning class and class struggles, state and revolution, and the dictatorship of the proletariat were introduced in China and had a great influence on the study of political science in China. Until 1949, many universities in China established departments of political science that trained personnel in the field. As a result, a number of well-known experts in political science emerged, and many valuable monographs on political science were published. In 1949, the People's Republic of China was founded. From then on, great importance was placed on learning from the Soviet Union's experiences in building socialism. China's higher education was also adjusted to follow the example of the Soviet Union. Unfortunately, there were no departments of political science in the universities of the Soviet Union, nor was there an independent research institute in its Academy of Sciences. Political teaching and research were combined with the study of law. For instance, the Soviet Universities' departments of law offered courses such as "Theory of State and Law" and "History of State and Law." Therefore, based on the blueprint of the Soviet Union, political science departments in China's universities were abolished in 1952. The affected teachers and courses were then merged into the departments of law. Political science in China no longer existed as an independent branch of learning. It was not until the third plenum of the 11th Congress of the Chinese Communist Party (CCP) in 1978, when the ten-year period of national turmoil known as the cultural revolution came to an end, that political science was restored in China as an independent subject.

This chapter will mainly discuss the restoration process in political science in China since 1980, as well as describe the present situation.

RESTORATION OF POLITICAL SCIENCE

After 1978, China's social sciences entered a new era of resurgence and development. Political science was once again emphasized as a course of study. In a speech in 1979, Deng Xiaoping stated, "For many years we have neglected the study of political science, law, sociology and world politics, and now we must hurry to make up our deficiencies in these subjects" (Deng, 1983, 188).

Meanwhile, the study of political science faced the challenge of solving the problems that emerged while trying to bring about socialist modernization. Under these circumstances, the study of political science in China was restored and began to develop.

The restoration of political science in China is marked by the beginning of the reconstruction of the Chinese Association of Political Science (CAPS), first established in 1932 in Nanjing. One of the founders, Professor Qian Duan-sheng, became the honorary chairman of the restored CAPS in 1980. Among the older generation of political scientists who took an active part in the original CAPS activities, most remained in mainland China after 1949, including well-known scholars such as Qian Duan-sheng, Zhang Xi-ruo, Qian Chang-zhao, Zhou Geng-sheng, Xu De-heng, and Wang Tie-ya. In 1952, when the colleges and universities were adjusted, the teaching and research of political science and of the science of law were combined; the Chinese Association of Political Science and Law (CAPSL) was founded in Beijing in April 1953. All of the older generation of political scientists who had remained in mainland China joined the association. Its first chairman was Dong Bi-wu, who had participated in the UN conference in San Francisco in April 1945 as one of the Chinese representatives. Professor Zhang You-yu, the former chairman of the restored CAPS, and the late professor Qian Duan-sheng, once the honorary chairman, both served as vice-chairman of the CAPSL. Professor Xu De-heng and Zhou Geng-sheng, once members of the CAPS, were also executive members of the CAPSL. After 1978, when China decided to differentiate between political science and law, and to develop each of them as an independent branch of learning, the CAPS and the Chinese Association of Law were both reestablished.

In December 1980, the inaugural meeting of the CAPS was held in Beijing. More than 150 scholars and cadres came from twenty-four provinces, municipalities, and autonomous regions throughout China, excluding the remote border provinces, to attend this inaugural meeting. The conference approved a "Five-Year (1981–1985) National Program of Political Science Research" and also determined the future direction and mission of the study of political science in China.

The program can be summarized as follows: The study of political science in China should be under the guidance of Marxism-Leninism, follow the principle of combining theory with practice, implement the policy of letting one hundred schools of thought contend, and affirm the scientific attitude of seeking truth from the facts. As to the area of research, first of all, creative research on the issue of socialist political systems and practical political problems in China should be undertaken, for example, the issues of system reform, various legislation including the problems of executive legislation, the relations between the state and the political party, and the problem of socialist democracy and its legal system. Not only should China's practical political problems be researched, but also foreign countries, East or West, big or small, should be studied. All that is good about foreign countries, including the fields of political systems, political life, and executive management, should be learned, absorbed, and used by the Chinese.

The conference emphasized research in the following six fields: (1) basic theoretical problems of political science; (2) problems related to the Chinese socialist political system; (3) contemporary foreign political systems and political doctrines; (4) the history of Chinese political thought and political systems; (5) the history of foreign political thought and political systems; and (6) international relations and issues in world politics.

After the CAPS was established, various provinces, municipalities, and autonomous regions throughout China also formed independent local associations. These areas included Heilongjiang, Jilin, Anhui, Shaanxi, Jiangsu, Henan, Guangxi, Sichuan, Shanghai, Tianjin, Beijing, and Chongqing. Up to the present, there have been about seventeen local political associations. In 1984, the CAPS joined the International Political Science Association and became one of its collective members. In July 1985, the CAPS sent representatives to attend the 13th World Congress of the International Political Science Association (IPSA) held in Paris. Professor Zhao Baoxu was elected an executive member of the IPSA. At the 14th Congress of IPSA, held in August 1988 in Washington, Hu Qian, one of China's professors of political science, assumed the post previously held by Zhao and became one of the executive members.

After the establishment of the CAPS and the local associations, various seminars on political science were held for academic exchanges both at home and abroad. The academic activities related to political science were increasing rapidly. Soon after, the Institute of Political Science, part of the Chinese Academy of Social Sciences, and some local academies of social science were set up, and a number of academic magazines on political science were published.

After the reestablishment of the study of political science in China, more than ten influential universities—Peking University, Fudan University, Jilin University, China Politics and Law University, Nanjing University, Xiamen University, Zhengzhou University, Zhongshan University, Nankai University, Wuhan University, Yunan University, Hebei University, and Huadong (East China) Normal University—set up political science departments, which train both undergraduate and graduate students in political science. Since the first publication of the book *Introduction to Political Science*, published by Peking University in 1982, more than ten textbooks of a similar nature have been published. Furthermore, many works focusing on various topics have also been published. The study of political science in China has gradually entered into a stage of prosperous development.

CURRENT STATUS OF POLITICAL SCIENCE

Thirteen years have passed since the restoration of the study of political science in China in 1980. In these years, the study of political science in China has made great progress.

First of all, because the Marxist-Leninist principle of "seeking truth from facts," the basic principle required to carry out all tasks effectively, is emphasized by the country and the Party Central Committee, and because of the progressive results achieved from the discussion throughout the country under the heading "Social Practice Is the Only Measure of Truth," China became alive, the economy became alive, and scientific inquiry and the study of political science flourished.

Like other fields of social science, political science research in China adheres to the guiding ideology of Marxism-Leninism, the principle of combining theory with practice, the policy of letting a hundred flowers blossom and a hundred schools of thought contend, as well as a practical and realistic style of work. Although the guiding ideology has not changed, there has been a marked improvement in practicing these principles. In recent years, scholars in their academic research are working to overcome the former rigid and dogmatic attitude toward Marxism-Leninism. Now, instead of following these outdated approaches—which gave only explanatory notes to the classical works of Marxism-Leninism, merely explained the present policy of the party, or were simply a propaganda—scholars strive to make practical and creative study on the basis of real materials and data obtained via the scientific method of investigation. That is, this method should try to act in accord with realistic conditions instead of blindly adhering to ideology, to take the general principles of Marxism-Leninism (such as the following: all matters are constantly in a state of flux, both related to and limited by one another; superstructure is determined by economic basis; the relations of production should be suited to the level of productive forces; and the people are the primary actors in historical development) as the guiding line but remain free from the trammels of some concrete classical Marxist-Leninist conclusion, which might not be in accord with the present actual situation. In the summer of 1989, the Party Central Committee wrote in a guiding document, "In theoretical work, we should, under the guidance of Marxism-Leninism, study in depth the new problems that arise in building modernization; continue to implement the policy of 'letting a hundred flowers blossom and a hundred schools of thought contend,' encourage the emancipation of mind, boldly exploring, putting forward various new ideas and solutions; and permit inavoidable faults in exploration and reserving different views" (Document of Central Committee 1989).

I think this guiding ideology is very wise. Without encouraging exploration and creation, it is impossible to get scientific conclusions or effective solutions for the many questions that may arise in practice. And without a suitable political environment to encourage scholars to explore and create boldly, scientific study can never be very dynamic. As a matter of fact in the past thirteen years, the inappropriate propaganda and demonstrations that were intended to pander to the temporary political situation have appeared less frequently in the works published by scholars of political science. Nowadays one can see quite a number of works and essays that dare to face reality—without avoiding discussion of social evils, analysis of sensitive problems, or speaking the truth. For instance, in recent years, monographs and articles discussing problems of corruption and anticorruption have been continually published. And from time to time, one can see works of real knowledge and deep insight.

Second, since the guiding ideology was gradually brought into order out of chaos, the study of political science in China, combined with a general trend toward a stable political environment, has led to important breakthroughs, including the following five.

1. After refuting the ultra-leftist "continuing revolution under the dictatorship of the proletariat," which once guided the cultural revolution, people reinterpreted the definition of class and the problems of the developing trend of class struggle in socialist society. They also demonstrated the existence and significance of other complicated social contradictions in socialist countries.

2. As to the problems facing the nation, scholars have abandoned the long-held, one-sided view that took the state as a tool for class repression and have spent a lot of time studying the administrative functions of the state as an administrative apparatus of public rights in society. Scholars have pointed out that the transformation of the prerevolution state apparatus into a nation led by the dictatorship of the proletariat cannot be completed in one step. This requires a long historical process in order to nurture what is useful or healthy and discard what is not.

3. Introducing political power as a new approach to the study of political science in China has prompted a series of changes. These include shifts from static to dynamic studies, from qualitative studies to integrating quantitative and qualitative studies, from macrocosmic to microcosmic studies, and from abstract value studies to economic studies.

4. As for the study of political development, that is, the study of how a nation is transformed from a traditional to a modern society, scholars have analyzed and summarized the modern experience of political development by using the research results of foreign countries. Meanwhile, scholars have also conducted fruitful research in the following fields: the influence of political power on political development; the relationship between developing democracy and maintaining political stability; the differentiation and coordination of social interests; political development; and political corruption.

5. For the development of social democracy, many new achievements have been made regarding the general characteristics of democracy and its implementation, comparisons between socialist democracy and capitalist democracy, the operating mechanism of socialist democracy, and the constitution and reformation of socialist democracy.

6. For the study of socialist political systems, scholars put forward the theory of multiparty coalition under the leadership of the Chinese Communist Party and demonstrated the role of the democratic parties in democratic consultation, in

democratic supervision, and in government and political affairs. This study is very significant in promoting China's socialist democracy and legal system.

In addition, the newer branches of learning in political science have also begun to make progress in such fields as political culture, political socialization, political sociology, political psychology, political anthropology, political broadcasting, and so on.

During the past thirteen years, along with the implementation of China's reform and open-door policy, the study of political science has also broken free and opened itself to the outside world; academic exchange with foreign countries in the area of political science has increased daily. The old days of rejecting all Western social science results, which had been branded as "bourgeois pseudoscience," have been significantly altered. Instead, it is now encouraged to assimilate all of the scientific and cultural results of all nations. Anything that is advanced, scientific, and suitable for China can be used by the Chinese. Therefore, many new results of political science in foreign countries have been gradually introduced into China. Some of the new Western schools of thought and theoretical systems in political science—such as behavioralism, postbehavioralism, analytic systems theory, and structural-functionalism—have been embraced by Chinese political scholars.

Third, in the past years, the study of political science in China has integrated more closely with "realistic politics." Thirteen years ago, after Deng Xiaoping initiated the reform of the political system and put forward the strategic target for constructing socialist democratic politics, China's social science workers began to place more emphasis on the new situation and practical problems that emerged in social political life. Chinese political scientists made many efforts to solve the practical problems of research work, such as system reform, mechanism reform, public administration, and democracy and the legal system. This trend can be seen clearly by briefly listing some topics of national seminars held in recent years by the CAPS: In January 1983, "Reform of Government Organization and the Cadre System"; in March 1985, "The International Environment for China's Four Modernizations Construction Policy in the late 1980s"; in June 1986, the functions of the government. These topics covered such issues as construction of socialist political power, socialist democracy and its system, the cadre system, the party's leadership, the system of the People's Congress, the election system, and the relationship between the central and local governments.

The concentration of realistic political problems also resulted in the change of methods used in this research. One can see a clear trend away from excessively theoretical inquiries toward a method of inquiry characterized by conducting social research and gathering data that can be scrutinized in a more scientific fashion. For example, in the seventh national five-year plan, there was a project proposed for social science study, an inquiry of the reform of the Chinese political system. To carry out this research, scholars from eleven universities worked together, with these universities spread all over China, including Beida, Fudan, Zhongshan, Wuda, Suda, Nanjing, and Tianjing Normal universities. I was in charge of this project. Crucial problems concerning the present political system reform needed to be addressed, and systematic investigations and analysis needed to be made. So each coordinated unit organized teachers and graduate students to make observations in some political area throughout the country by visiting, having informal discussions, conducting surveys, and presenting case studies. In the first year, we investigated the problems of the People's Congress in local areas, from the elections of representatives to their personal political and cultural quality, their consciousness of political participation, their value attendance, their working style, and their relationship with the electorate. This investigation was conducted from Guangdong in South China to Jilin in North China, from Jiangsu in East China to Henan, Hebei in North China.

On the basis of firsthand scientific data obtained from the nationwide investigation, we issued eighteen reports. Then we held a discussion attended by scholars and personnel of the local NPC (among them were four secretary generals of the People's Congress in the cities investigated). We also made this discussion a basis for an advisory report (including the actual situation, the existing problems, and ways of improving them) for leading authorities to use as a reference for decision making. The following year we made a nationwide investigation on the separation of the party and the administration in the Chinese political system reform. The results of the investigations, consisting of two collections of reports, were published by China's Shannxi People's Press in 1990: *Democratic Politics and Local People's Congress* (Collection of Survey Reports); *Governmental Institutions and the Functions of the Communist Party* (Collection of Survey Reports).

For a long time, the development of political science in China experienced setback after setback. There seems to be a law working here: the closer the development of a social science is to the current political situation, the more likely is interference by "current politics." Political science is a branch of learning closely related to realistic politics. Therefore, political science is the most difficult type of research to conduct. The recent development of all this political science research has come as a result of the practical necessity to conduct such research. At present, China's reform of both the economic and the political systems is a revolutionary change toward complementing the socialist system with Chinese characteristics. This reform is concerned with politics, economics, culture, and ideological fields and will come into contact with many layers of society. In the course of this great change, there will likely be all sorts of unexpected problems, to which political scientists can offer scientific and effective solutions. This will supply a necessary precondition for the progression of political science in China. Therefore, no matter how difficult the environment may be, I believe that in the future the study of political science in China is bound to enter a more vigorous, practical, and realistic phase.

REFERENCES

Deng Xiaoping. 1983. *Selected Works of Deng Xiaoping (1975–1982)*. Beijing: Foreign Languages Press, p. 188.

Document of the Central Committee of the Communist Party of China. 1989. Issue 17.
    Beijing.
Li Jing-peng. 1988. "The Ten Years of Political Science Study." *Theoretical Information*
    177, (November 14). Beijing.
"Political Science" volume of *Encyclopedia of China*. 1992. Beijing: China Publishing
    House.
Zhao Baoxu. 1984. The Revival of Political Science in China." *Political Science* (Fall).

PART II

Specific Policy Problems

CHAPTER 3

Reforming the Social Security System in China

Peter Nan-shong Lee

As Peter Nan-shong Lee discusses in this chapter, the social security system in the People's Republic of China is extremely broad and includes a range of concerns. Lee concentrates mainly on retirement pensions, health services, and housing, all of which have registered a visible increase in spending since 1979. This increased welfare spending has been attributed to a "peace dividend" based on the normalization of relations with the West and the former Soviet Union.

Lee explores the changing scope and modes of state intervention within the Chinese social security system on the basis of three program areas: retirement pensions, health service, and housing in the urban area. All three have undergone varying degrees of "privatization" in terms of the marketization (or commercialization) of benefits and services and the transfer of ownership from the state sector to the collective and private sectors. This policy trend has been coupled with organizational stream-lining and managerial innovations. The pace and extent of this privatization tendency have been dictated by a variety of factors particular to China. The end results are marked by interesting mixes of the state hierarchy and market mechanisms.

Pensions reflect various policy considerations: first, that many people were overdue for retirement; second, that many had worked beyond the normal retirement age; third, that a bulge of aged populations would appear by the year 2030; and fourth, that improvement of the living standards made the general population more aware of retirement. The local government has unified management of the pension funds contributed by the enterprise under their unification. Since 1984, 80 percent of Chinese retirement systems in the urban sector have been restored. Rural families in particular were sensitive to retirement systems, since they had been compelled to accept birth control. However, the retirement problem of rural families has yet to be solved.

There is a fixed ratio of total wages to collection of retirement funds. Second, pensions fall into stable and controllable retirement payments, including subsidies for grain, food, funeral, and death. Less stable items, such as medical care, are still sustained by the enterprise. Employees are encouraged to seek additional pension benefits, including commercial social security. The precondition to unified management is that the agencies have the necessary skill to invest and nurture the public contributions.

Considering public hospitals, a key problem not unknown to the United States is that the revenue of the hospital is constantly lower than the actual cost, and thus there is inadequate compensation for services. The anti-intellectual trend for 1958 to 1976 labeled physicians, technical workers, and nurses as intellectuals, which devastated the field. The hospital system was also hindered by an absence of younger, well-trained physicians. Such recruitment as well as morale problems, according to Lee, have been alleviated by recognizing that compensation should be commensurate with training and skill. As soon as these initial difficulties were overcome, the health service reform was carried out by introducing the "contractual responsibility system," which was adapted from the industrial sector, together with an effort to rationalize the pricing of health services.

In describing housing, Lee suggests that considerable housing has been added, with one-third of all housing constructed between 1979 and 1989. There are administrative implications to the in-kind approach to services, since this form of income distribution is neither explicit nor consistent. Housing is allocated based on egalitarianism, seniority, rank, and efficiency, not to mention availability. Because housing units are not permitted to be objects of commercial transaction, rent is artificially low and heavily subsidized. The construction industry has been regarded as a form of consumption rather than production. As Lee suggests, the housing reform in China has pointed to the direction that housing subsidies will be eliminated and the pay structure readjusted so that employees can afford the full market value of their housing benefits.

This chapter suggests that the privatization trend as such has been able to overcome initial ideological difficulties, and to extend the application of economic leverage and market mechanism to the realm of the distribution and provision of the social security benefits. However, the further progress of the policy trend appears to rest on the success of restructuring the framework of the command economy and, ultimately, the improvement of efficiency and productivity of society.

China has been involved in a privatization movement with enormous magnitude, and for more than a decade since the late 1970s the movement partly overlapped the similar efforts made by British Prime Minister Margaret Thatcher and U.S. President Ronald Reagan. The scope of privatization embraces not only the property right dimension (i.e., ownership privatization) comparable to the British case, but also the marketization of services and benefits similar to the American case. For quite a while, Chinese ideologues would still frown on the notion of privatization for its imported meaning from capitalism but, in practice, Chinese policymakers are confronted with such policy problems as the oversized state hierarchy, unbearable financial burden, and excessive administrative load of the government. In practical terms, Chinese policymakers should share a common language with their Western counterparts. In the same vein as noted above, this chapter will try to identify the key issues of the privatization movement in China, and to monitor the progress of its first decade from 1979 to 1989.

The concept of *social security* refers broadly to an aggregate of benefits and services provided by public organizations, including the government, to meet the contingencies and basic needs of members of society. Given China's level of economic development, the coverage of social security is extensive, and the number of programs is considerable.[1] The programs include, for example, retirement pensions, birth control allowances, sick leave and benefits, health care insurance, disability insurance, allowances to dependents on death, unemployment insurance, collective amenities, cultural facilities, housing benefits, subsidies, social relief, and disaster relief. This chapter represents an endeavor to identify and examine some common features of the reforms of China's social security system and to compare its variations across selected programs during the period from 1979 to 1989. For analytical purposes, this paper shall focus on retirement pensions, health services, and housing benefits.

Authors in China and in the West tend to agree that the overall investment in the several programs of social security was stagnant from the 1950s to the 1970s.[2] However, there has been considerable growth of spending in such areas as housing, medical care subsidies, and "collective welfare" of enterprise units since the 1970s.[3] The official sources have vaguely attributed this increase in spending to the need to repay the "debt" that the state owed to the employees of enterprises, government officials, teachers, and veteran revolutionaries. Yet information is not sufficient to shed light on this major change of policy priority. It is plausible to explain the above-mentioned increase of welfare spending as "peace dividends" for the People's Republic of China on the arrival of an era of peace and normalization with the West and the Soviet Union.

Another factor for the larger expenditure in social security benefits might relate to the demand of workers and staff members in enterprise units for the improvement of the living standard, especially during the reform era, but such demand cannot be met through the regular adjustments of the standard wage scales. In other words, the increase of welfare is taken as an avenue for the improvement of workers' and staff members' incomes and for the alleviation of their material hardship if wage increments are not feasible. For example, when the standard wage increment was set aside during the Gang of Four era in 1975, collective welfare increased to sustain the living standard of workers and staff in the state-owned enterprises (Lee and Chow 1987). Also in the 1980s, when the State Council imposed restrictions on the increase of wages and bonuses, welfare was taken as a loophole to improve material benefits of employees in industrial enterprises. This has been done especially in those enterprise units with a large share of retained profit (Tong and Qian 1985; Huang and Yang 1987).

The increase in social security spending has not been limited to the industrial sector and state-owned enterprises. Since the 1970s, attention has been drawn not only to the social security issues in the agricultural sector but also to those of the collective-owned enterprises in the urban area.[4] The provision of social security benefits was, in the past, hierarchically structured among various segments of society, just as was the pattern of wage distribution (Ahmand and Hussain 1989). That is to say, those sectors/strata of the population that did not fall into the list of policy priorities of technology, heavy industry, and defense strength tended to end up on the lower wage scales and therefore received lower levels of social security provisions. The gradual phasing out of the war economy has relaxed the resource constraints. This change will very likely lead to a readdressing of the disparities of social security provisions between the industrial and agricultural sectors and between the state-owned and collective-owned industries.

There have been several meaningful approaches to the study of the social security system at various organizational levels and in different sectors of the population in China. For instance, an economic approach treats social security as an integral component of the pay structure (Wong 1989; Lee 1988); sociological treatments tackle the subject in terms of human interactions in the basic units (e.g., the patron-client relationship), community in the workplace, and the culture of authority and dependency (Whyte and Parish 1984; Walder 1986; Davis 1988). In addition, the social security system can be studied from a political dimension focusing on the conflict and articulation of interests involving industrial workers, enterprise units, and various governmental echelons (Shirk 1985; White 1983; Walder 1987). As an alternative, this paper will analyze welfare systems as a subject of public organization and management. Our discussion will concentrate on the following questions: How is public power exercised in providing benefits and services to the members of society? Through which organizational forms and with what managerial tools is the Chinese social security system administered? What have been the tendencies and key objectives of social security reforms since the mid 1980s? How successful have they been?

China's social security system has experienced phenomenal growth in the post-Mao era but it still cannot meet the drastic increase of demand of the population. This increase is partly responsible for the pressure for the reforms that began in the 1980s. The Chinese policymakers have tried a wide range of institutional and managerial alternatives in attacking the inadequacies of the social security system. On top of organizational streamlining (or "rectification"), the economic approaches—such as cost management, the restructuring of fee collection, reasonable pricing systems, and the market mechanisms—have been introduced. This chapter represents an attempt to assess the use and limitations of the market approach in the recent reforms in China.

Evidence suggests that the restructuring of China's social security system has been influenced by the reforms in other sectors of society. For example, in the functional area of retirement pensions, an attempt has been made to increase the centralization of power from the enterprise level to the state level (especially the local government level) and to rely more heavily on state intervention to transfer income from one generation to another and to spread the financial burden and uncertainty to a larger geographical area and a greater size of population. In the area of health services, the programs of "rectification" and the "contractual responsibility system" have been borrowed from the industrial sector. In addition, attempts have been made to strengthen cost management and to rationalize the pricing system of the health service system. Finally, it appears that economic approaches are mainly employed to tackle the provision of housing benefits, such as the restructuring of the rental systems and the introduction of house-purchasing schemes.

The selection of alternatives in the reforms of China's social security system is related to the pertinent merits of the market mechanisms and the state hierarchy as well as the trends of "denationalization" (or "privatization") in different country contexts. All three program areas (i.e., retirement pensions, health services, and housing) involve, in varying degrees, measurable outputs, divisible costs, and marketable benefits, according to Anthony Downs's (1967) conceptualization. Except for part of the health service system, such as preventive care and immunization, all three program areas are concerned with the type of benefits and services that are excludable and can be enjoyed on an individual basis (Ostrom 1977). In terms of technical feasibility, it should not be difficult for the market mechanisms to substitute for the state hierarchy in provision and delivery.

However, the failings of the state hierarchy are as prevalent as the limitations of the market mechanisms. Thus, the weaknesses of the administrative means do not necessarily amount to the strengths of the economic (or market) approaches. In concrete terms, where does the balance between the state hierarchy and the market mechanisms rest in the reforms of China's social security system? How successful have the economic approaches been in substituting for the state hierarchy? In organizational terms, is the "withering away" of the state inevitable insofar as these three program areas are concerned? These are some broad theoretical questions that will guide this study of reforms in program areas such as retirement, pensions, health services, and housing benefits in post-Mao China.

THE PROVISION OF RETIREMENT BENEFITS

Soon after the establishment of the PRC, the first pension scheme for industrial workers and staff members was put forth jointly by the Ministry of Labor and the All China Federation of Labor Unions when, in February 1951, the "Regulations of Labor Insurance of the PRC" was promulgated, with immediate effect.

Subsequently, between 1953 and 1956, several amendments to the 1951 "Regulations" were made to expand its scope of application to include the construction industry and commercial units and to improve the level of payments from 35-60 percent to 50-70 percent of the standard wages. By 1956, approximately 94 percent of employees in the state-owned enterprises, state-private jointly owned enterprises, and private-owned enterprises were covered by the retirement pension system (Qiu and Shi 1985).

In the meantime, a number of directives and regulations were announced to provide retirement benefits to the civil servants, party cadres, and members of other public organizations. These were coupled with allowances for the dependents of those who died during the war (December 1952, amended in 1953 and 1955) and for medical care for officials and cadres (September 1952, amended in 1954 and 1955). In general, the social security benefits that the civil servants and cadres enjoyed (including retirement pensions) were comparable to those provided to industrial workers and staff members (Qiu and Shi 1985).

In accordance with the 1951 "Regulations of Labor Insurance of the PRC," the retirement funds for workers and staff members in state-owned enterprises were under "unified management" (*tong cou*) by the All China Federation of Labor Unions, together with its local branches and its branches in various trades (such as communication, railway, etc.). Each enterprise unit was then required to contribute 3 percent of its total wage bill, and the funds raised were paid to the retired workers and staff members (Cong 1986; Feng 1986). The organizational scale of the All China Federation of Labor Unions, with its branches, was large enough to build a financial pool and thus to maintain a balance between those enterprise units that overdrew from their accounts and those that spent less than their contribution. As an extension of the party-state, the All China Federation enjoyed credibility and trust and possessed sufficient organizational strength and leadership to administer the retirement pensions.

However, the branches of the All China Federation were badly assaulted by the Red Guards and were subsequently abolished during the cultural revolution. As a consequence, from 1966 onward, there was no longer an institution responsible for the management and provision of retirement benefits. In November 1969, the Military Control Committee of the Ministry of Finance issued a circular to delegate the managerial power over retirement benefits to the enterprise level and to pay pension to pensioners from the "nonbusiness expenditure" accounts of the enterprise units. Additionally, a considerable number of applications for retirement in both governmental departments and industrial enterprises were held up until the early 1980s (Qiu and Shi 1985).

A number of factors contributed to the listing of the retirement pensions on the policy agenda in China. First, those employees in industrial and governmental sectors who had been held up for applications were overdue for their retirement as the country recovered from the cultural revolution. Second, the age cohort of those government officials and party cadres who had joined the revolution before 1949 had already been extended long beyond their retirement age. Third, the early indication of a rapidly aging population had begun to manifest itself in some areas by the early 1980s, for instance in Shanghai, and it was envisaged that the peak of an aged population would arrive by 2030 (Feng 1986). Finally, the improvement of the living standard in both rural and urban areas made the general population more aware of the need for social security, especially retirement pensions. Besides the lack of retirement, the need for financial arrangement was keenly felt when the rural families were persuaded to accept birth control ("Jainshe juyou . . ." 1989). The aged in Chinese rural society rely heavily on their male offspring for their security during old age.

The process of reorganization of the retirement pensions was activated by the introduction of the profit retention system in 1979. It was required that pension payments be charged to the accounts of retained profit (instead of to those of "non-business expenditure" (Zhuang and Li 1985). The new accounting procedure entailed new ways to allocate values among groups of people, among enterprise units, and between enterprise units and the state. At that time, the workers and staff members felt that the pension payments tended to cut into their share of retained profit. Those enterprise units that had a greater proportion of retirees felt burdened by the large share of pension payments coupled with correspondingly reduced retained profit (Zhuang and Li 1985; Tong and Qian 1984). In addition, it has been a general consensus during the reform era that the enterprise units should concentrate on production and management and that retirement pensions and other social functions (e.g., day-care centers, health care, etc.) should be entrusted to the government at various levels (Liu Li-li 1987). In other words, the consensus is that the enterprise units are required to contribute to the accumulation of pension funds but are not expected to administer them directly.

The reform of the retirement pension systems features the centralization of managerial power from the enterprise level to the local government level. In retrospect, the 1969 decision to entrust the enterprise units to handle the retirement benefits was made on an *ad hoc* basis because most of the public organizations, including central ministries, local governments, and labor unions, could not operate properly under the circumstances of the cultural revolution. Therefore, the pension reform should partly be taken as an effort to return from the *ad hoc* arrangements made since 1969 (Tong and Qian 1984; Ahmand and Hussain 1989). However, the reform of the pension systems has in general followed the residential principle in administering retirement funds. That is, each local government is given principal responsibility for the "unified management" (*tong cou*) of the pension funds contributed by the enterprise units under its jurisdiction, and each functions as a financial pool to ensure the balance between contributions and payments of enterprise units in the long run (Zhuang and Li 1985).

In most cases of "unified management" of retirement pensions, municipal authorities and local governments at the county or township level have been given main power and responsibility. Fujian was reportedly the first provincial government to take charge of the "unified management" of retirement pension funds (Ding 1988). As a rule, a new administrative unit (or bureau) is created at the appropriate level of the government to handle matters related to "unified management." By and large, those centrally run enterprises are assigned to the local government with regard to their affiliation in the retirement schemes. In addition to this residential principle, "unified management" is structured along functional lines in some exceptional cases, such as railway system, postal service, or communications.

The restoration of the retirement pension systems has been relatively extensive and fast since 1984. It is estimated that the "unified management" of retirement pension schemes has been restored to or established in approximately 80 percent of the counties and townships across China. It is reported that some forms of retirement pensions have been introduced to an entire province or municipality, such as Beijing, Shanghai, Tientsin, Hebei, Guangdong, Jiangxi, Fujian, Henan, Anhui, Shangdong, Shaanxi, and Jilin (Shi 1988). My field trip to Henan province in 1989 confirms the press reports about the extensiveness of implementation. In the municipalities, counties, and townships I visited in August 1989, all—without exception—had their pension system reestablished. In addition, my interviews in various localities also confirmed that those collective-owned enterprises and commercial units in both urban and rural areas have been covered for the first time by some form of retirement benefits for their employees. Moreover, the contract workers have been given not only medical care benefits but also retirement benefits in order to enhance the appeal of the contractual hiring system, one of the major aspects of the economic reform in the PRC (White 1987).

Several characteristics of the reform of the retirement pension systems deserve our attention. First, the collection of the retirement funds is based on a fixed ratio of the total wage bill coupled with a percentage of retained profit, presumably considering both the financial strength of an enterprise unit and the actual need of the pensioners (Shi 1988). Second, for the time being, pensions paid fall into only those stable, controllable, and basic categories such as retirement payment, subsidy to grain price, subsidy to supplementary food, subsidy to funeral and death expenses, subsidy to cadres on long leave, and special allowance, but less-stable and controllable items, such as medical care, are still shouldered by the enterprise units (Shi 1988). As expected, the bills for medical benefits will grow larger as the population becomes increasingly older. Third, with a very modest beginning, workers and staff members are encouraged to seek pension benefits through other channels, including commercial social security schemes on top of the minimum security net provided by the "unified management" of the local governments (Cui 1988).

The successful "unified management" of retirement benefits hinges on a basic condition, that is, the knowledge and skill to handle large funds, as well as the effective channels of investment. The existing discussions in China have already covered the issue of a high inflation rate, which might encroach on the accumulated pension funds (Gao 1988; Ding, 1988). It is equally apparent that risk would be high if there were no reliable and profitable channels of investment to ensure the growth of the pension funds. Otherwise, the state has to shoulder the burden for the depletion of pension funds because of inflation.

THE DELIVERY OF HEALTH SERVICES

The health service in China is administered and provided by the public organizations rather than the private organizations, that is, public hospitals, their supervising authorities, and financial appropriating units. Since the state-owned public hospitals are not managed much differently from the governmental units and enterprise units, it is not surprising that the initial phase of readjustment of the health service was visibly influenced by the similar efforts of organizational streamlining in the governmental and industrial sectors.

The deficiencies of the Chinese health service are seen as more organizational than economic in nature. A Chinese analyst made the following diagnosis:

The managerial power over the hospitals is overly concentrated in the hands of the state apparatus, and thus the hospitals are deprived of vitality because of the excessive and rigid way of state intervention; all the medical functions and programs are dictated by simple administrative orders and political mobilization, and they are denied needed economic motivation; all items of expenditure are paid by the state through so called "unified payment and collection" [of medical expenditure]; the revenue of the hospital is made constantly lower than the actual cost in both manpower and material sense, and as a result, cost cannot be compensated through the charges for the service. This has created a situation in which the hospital becomes economically irresponsible, and negligent of economic accounting, coupled with impairments to economic efficiency and social effect and serious waste in financial, material, and human resources. . . . This economic system has deprived the hospital of the motivation, vitality, and needed pressure and thereby has posed restrictions on its further developments. (Du, Xie, and He 1985, translation supplied)

The major thrust of the health service reform started with an endeavor to improve the pay of medical doctors, technicians, and nurses, along with other "intellectuals." The category of "intellectuals" (doctors, teachers, engineers, and researchers) was devastated during the radical politics and the anti-intellectual trend from 1958 to 1976. Another major reform initiative concentrated on the task of "rectification," that is, making new regulations, clearly defining responsibility, refining job descriptions, and training junior doctors and nurses (Yan 1985). This endeavor was an integral part of Deng Xiaoping's overall strategy of organizational streamlining since 1975 (with interruptions during 1976–77).

In a manner comparable to that in the governmental sector, considerable energy was devoted to rebuilding the leadership team in the hospital administration. In an effort to reorganize the leadership team and to cultivate a new generation of "professionalized, knowledgeable, young and revolutionalized" cadres, caution was taken in order to retain experienced doctors until the new medical students were available due to acute shortages of medical manpower. It was not until the mid 1980s that the medical establishment began to institutionalize the policy package of leadership rejuvenation, as well as retirement and long leave for cadres at age sixty for males and fifty-five for females. As a result, the average age for doctors and hospital administrators dropped; for instance, at Xie-He Hospital in

Beijing, it fell from fifty-two to fifty during 1983–86. The medical establishment also borrowed the technique of reorganization from the industrial sector by introducing an appointment system through application and competition, especially for the heads of departments and offices. This appointment system helped weed out the less desirable personnel and recruit better-qualified doctors and administrators (Beijing xiehe . . . 1986).

Another area of reform in the health service system is concerned with the following paradox: on the one hand, there were complaints of overconcentration of power in the relationship of the supervising authorities to the hospital units; on the other hand, the supervising authorities found it very difficult to enforce financial criteria in the hospital units. To overcome this paradox, a form of the "contractual responsibility system" was borrowed from the industrial enterprises, giving economic concessions to the hospital units for their attempts to practice thrift and to save money. The hospital unit was given managerial power over the "supplementary fund," which covers its day-to-day expenses, excluding expensive repair and procurement of large equipment and facilities. Additionally, the hospital unit was allowed to retain a percentage of the supplementary fund in proportion to the amount of money that it saved or the total deficit that it cut. The retained share can be used as subsidies to salaries, as floating wages, or as incentive payments to staff members and doctors. It can be used for development projects as well. For each category of the hospital performances, a set of quotas and evaluating schemes was introduced (Yan Huizhang 1985; "Shixing jingji . . ." 1981; Du 1989; "Guanyu weisheng . . ." 1985).

The health service reform has gone beyond the administrative reorganization and decentralization of power by injecting an additional ingredient of economic orientation. However, before this economic orientation was translated into concrete policy proposals an ideological redefinition of the nature of the health service was required. This did take place starting from the mid-1980s: the health service was redefined as one form of sophisticated manual labor, and thus medical personnel, including doctors, were to be paid at a level commensurate with their training, skills, and jobs. According to the view of "Socialism at its initial stage" and the restoration of the "commodity economy," the health service is treated as a component of the tertiary economy, and its allocation is subject to the channel of commercial transactions. Accordingly, the viewpoint that the health service is one form of free welfare was refuted, and this prepared the way for the pricing and financial reforms in the health service (Li 1985).

Minister of Health, Chen Mingzheng, summarized the main features of the health service reform as follows. First, the individual doctors, collectives, and corporations should be permitted to practice medicine, although the state-run hospitals are still to be given the main role. In public hospitals, doctors should be allowed to practice medicine during their spare time, and their overtime services are to be compensated. Second, although the excessive and indiscriminate increase of medical fees ought to be prohibited, all the charges to the medical service are to be brought to an appropriate level to cover the "basic costs" (excluding salaries and wages, and procurement and repairs for expensive items). By doing so, the hospital units and medical personnel can be properly supported, with the government's appropriation minimized. Third, a proper sense of investment in public health and medical care is to be promoted, and such investment should be appreciated in economic terms as well. Fourth, the concept of management and entrepreneurship is to be brought into the medical profession in order to improve revenue on the one hand and to reduce costs on the other (Chen 1989).

The health service reform has also been aimed at the curtailment of irregular practices. These irregularities resulted partly because the pay for medical personnel did not match the value of their services and because medical fees were set artificially lower than real costs. Consequently in this heavily subsidized system of health service, patients were often encouraged to demand excessively high quality service, for more expensive prescriptions than necessary, and for medication on behalf of their family members, because they do not have to pay for the service commensurate to its real value. These deviations were derived from the notion that one can acquire medical service free of charge or for less than its real value (Hu 1989). However, since the reform era, hospitals have practiced another type of abuse: charging unreasonably high fees for their services, at the expense of quality. Therefore, it is proposed to introduce a reasonable pricing system to make patients pay part of their expenses and thus to regulate their artificially high demand for medical care. Moreover, a reasonable pricing system can help facilitate the effective use of health services on the basis of the differences of quality and quantity and can help minimize abuse and irregularity (Chen 1989).

Nonetheless, it is still an objective of policymakers in China to retain some of the welfare characteristics in health services in spite of the economic and commercial orientation just noted. The State Council issued a directive in 1981 that the charges for labor insurance (for state-owned industrial enterprises) and for public insurance (for civil servants, cadres, teachers, etc.) should exclude labor costs. This means that the labor costs for health services ought to be paid through the state appropriation (Zhuang 1986). In subsequent reforms, it has been made clear that the state still intends to subsidize health services through its investments in expensive and large-scale equipment and facilities, as well as in repairs ("Guanyu weisheng . . ." 1985). In addition, the programs of immunization and preventive medicine have been heavily subsidized and in some cases are free of charge.

DISTRIBUTION OF HOUSING BENEFITS

On the eve of the establishment of the PRC in 1949, the property of the Chinese Nationalist (KMT) regime was confiscated by the new government. In the 1950s, a sizable number of housing units of the capitalists was seized by the government during the "Three-Anti" and "Five-Anti" campaign. Still more were taken by the regime through the "socialist reform" in housing and were subsequently administered by the "public-private joint management" and "unified management" of rental service during the middle 1950s. All housing units just mentioned constituted the available stock immediately after 1949 (Laurence 1981).

From 1949 to 1983, a considerable number of housing units was added to the existing stock, which is estimated at 927,070,000 square meters (living floor space, excluding kitchen, toilet, lobby, and staircase). During the reform era, the housing shortage has drawn the attention of the top policymakers. This reflects on the statistical data that one-third of the housing units in the PRC built in the entire period of 1949–89 were built during the decade between 1978 and 1987 (Su 1987).

The government officials, party cadres, and employees in enterprises do not normally purchase and own housing units. Instead, they rent the housing units, with a very low rental payment. Conceptually speaking, the low and actually subsidized rent of the employee is taken as one form of payment in kind in order to supplement the standard wage. The standard wage has been kept very low for several decades, since 1949 (Sun 1986). Some Chinese authors take this form of subsidized rent as a residual of the "supply system" of the Yenan period (1935–49), which has perpetuated to the present after the introduction of the standard wage scales in 1956 (Liu 1988). The practice of low rent has been reinforced by Marxist ideological legacy, which treats the subsidized rent as one form of public welfare. The Marxists and Communists in China, the Soviet Union, and East European countries do not in principle endorse a capitalist system, but they do not take exception to the fact that the standard wage, subsidized-rent, fringe benefits, and other welfare payments constitute an integral pay package in both socialist and capitalist societies (Liu 1988).

A pay package of the aforementioned design has some profound administrative implications. In effect, a sizable income has to be distributed in such forms as services, benefits, and payments in kinds through a complex administrative system involving multiple levels of hierarchy and numerous units of a public organization. The criteria for such a pattern of income distribution are numerous, vague, and not necessarily consistent among themselves. They include egalitarianism, seniority, rank, cost, efficiency, and resource constraints. Not only are most of these criteria difficult to operationalize and to measure, but also their relative weight cannot be readily determined in an objective fashion (Wang 1986). From time to time, the central policymakers have to assign greater weight to a particular group of people on the basis of some general observation of their need, for instance, the financial appropriation in December 1982 to alleviate housing shortages for schoolteachers ("Guowuyuan bangongting . . ." 1983). In 1983, the State Council, by a sense of fairness, legality, and egalitarianism, promulgated a set of regulations to control "excessive upgrading" of the housing standards for high cadres and officials ("Guowuyuan guanyu yange . . ." 1983). In 1984, when this set of regulations did not appear effective, the Disciplinary Inspection Committee of the Central Committee (CC), CCP, issued still another circular to prohibit the "misconduct" (or improper work style) of building and allocating excessively large and high-quality housing units for cadres themselves or for their relatives ("Renzhen quanche . . ." 1984).

On top of the issues of maladministration and quasi-corrupt behavior, there has been a problem of housing shortages, especially in urban China. A survey conducted in 1986 indicates that, on average, each individual is allocated 6.36 square meters of "living floor space" in urban China. This is estimated to less than one-half of the average for each person in the United States, Japan, Western Germany, the Soviet Union, Yugoslavia, or Romania by the standards of the 1970s. Approximately one-quarter of the urban population (or 10,540,000 households) are considered short of housing (meaning inadequate living floor space, overcongestion, and inconveniences); about 44 percent of households do not have running water, and 75 percent of households share toilets and baths. More than one-half of public housing need repairs. Other studies confirm the overall housing shortage in urban China (Wang 1986).

This general shortage of housing is attributed to several causes. The investment in housing remained relatively low between 1949 and 1978 for a variety of reasons, including the war economy under a hostile international environment, the "ultraleftist" emphasis on production versus consumption, and the lack of funding sources for housing projects other than state appropriation. Furthermore, since the mid 1950s, the housing policy of the CCP has had the adverse effect of inhibiting the participation of potential investors (such as enterprise units, collectives, individuals, and even local governments) in housing development projects (Cai 1987). In China the housing units are not allowed to be the object of commercial transactions, and the rent is artificially low and heavily subsidized. This housing policy makes other alternative investments more attractive. For example, the interest on bank deposits is often higher than rent. Thus, it does not pay for Chinese urban dwellers to purchase housing units rather than rent them. Additionally, the low-rent policy creates a constant burden for the state treasury to provide financial appropriation for the maintenance of housing units and the housing development projects (Zhang 1986).

The reform of housing policy has often been traced back to Deng Xiaoping's remarks to several central leaders on April 2, 1980. Deng suggested that the construction industry had long been neglected by policymakers in the PRC because it had been treated as one form of consumption rather than production. He stated that in the long term, the planning of the construction industry should be given an important place; it can generate revenue, increase capital, improve the employment problem, and meet the housing demand in cities. Therefore, he recommended a review of the housing policy, focusing on the construction and allocation of housing units. He lent support to home-purchasing schemes and rent adjustments. In Deng's view, rent should be adjusted to an appropriate level to make it profitable for residents to take part in home-purchasing schemes ("Deng Xiaoping's Talk" 1984). Zhao Ziyang, then premier and later secretary general of the party, reportedly played an important role in coordinating various pilot programs of housing policy reform, including the one in the Yendai municipality. The first policy proposal for urban housing reform in Yendai was endorsed by the State Council in July 1987. In February 1988, the Leadership Team of the

Housing Reform of the State Council put forth the "Draft-proposal for the Implementation of Housing Reform in Urban China."

The housing reform is a formidable task for the policymakers in China, requiring several phases in order to attain its ultimate objectives as suggested by Deng Xiaoping in 1980. The ultimate model features a direct economic interaction between the supplier and the consumer of housing benefits. This ultimate model differs from the existing practice, in which the consumer enjoys a housing benefit paid for or heavily subsidized by the third party, that is, the state. The ultimate model requires the consumer (i.e., the tenant or buyer) to pay in full to the supplier through rent or purchasing payments reflecting the market value of the housing unit. To enable the consumer to pay for his or her housing benefits, two aspects of reform are warranted: first, the housing subsidies (in hidden or open form) have to be eliminated entirely; and second, the pay structure of employees has to be readjusted upward so that they can afford to cover the full market value of their housing benefits, either through rental or purchasing arrangements (Cai 1987; Su 1987).

Beginning in August 1987, the pilot program of the Yendai municipality intends to raise the rent of housing units under its jurisdiction to the level of "cost rent," an amount equivalent to the cost (including depreciation, maintenance, managerial fee, interest from investment, and tax). The ultimate objective is the "commercial rent" (the level of rent that covers the cost, profit, tax, and value of the land). As the first step, all residents are required to pay "basic rent," estimated at 1.28 yen per square meter of living floor space, and this is higher than the average of the old rent (1.09). Accordingly, a compensation is given, in the form of rent vouchers, to make up the difference. Presumably, a future increase in wages would eventually absorb the rent increase. The old residents can use the vouchers to offset the increase in rent, and the new tenants can use the vouchers, together with their saving, to purchase houses if they do not want to rent housing units ("Guowuyuan guanyu tongyi . . ." 1988).

In the "Draft-proposal for the Implementation of Housing Reform in Urban China" (February 1988), the State Council underscored its main objective: to achieve the commercialization of housing and to enable residents to acquire the right of use and/or ownership of housing units through transactions rather than through administrative allocation. The state should increase wages of employees so that they can pay directly for their housing benefits. The state should eventually cease to subsidize employees through its financial appropriation for construction and maintenance of housing units and thus cease to maintain artificially low rent. The rent paid by tenants and the sum for home-purchasing schemes would eventually create a steady flow of capital and would inject money into the cycle of investment in which the real estate market, banks, construction industry, and developers all have a role to play. In addition, before the completion of the full-fledged reform of commercialization, those who enjoy greater housing benefits should pay proportionally more, and thus inequitable distribution of housing benefits can be curtailed ("Guowuyuan zhufang" 1988).

The 1988 draft-proposal of housing reform is legally based on the December 1983 regulations concerning the management of private housing. The 1983 regulations provide legal protections for the ownership of housing and rental benefits and also build a legal foundation for the functions and roles of the managerial agent of private housing in the absence of the owner ("Chengshi siyou . . ." 1983). The 1988 draft-proposal is also anchored in the 1984 circular, which concerns the sale of public housing units to private individuals on the basis of a series of pilot programs in Changzhou, Zhengzhou, Shashi, and Xiping ("Chengxiang jianche . . ." 1984). The 1988 draft-proposal therefore constitutes an intermediary stage toward a situation in which employees, with their improved wage level, can own their housing units, purchased from the public organizations or private development corporations on a fully commercial basis.

CONCLUSION

This chapter started with a theoretical concern about the use and abuse of the state hierarchy in the provision of social security benefits in China. The chapter then analyzed the possible movement toward the application of the economic approaches, including the market mechanisms, to various program areas. On the basis of the foregoing investigation, it appears that the role of the state has expanded in the area of retirement pensions but that the scope of state intervention has been narrowed down considerably in the provision of health services and housing benefits during the reform era. In fact, it is entirely possible for a development toward a full-scale privatization of housing in the PRC. On the whole, this study of China's social security reforms has produced a conclusion with mixed theoretical implications.

On the one hand, this chapter has lent validity to the view that the public organization is less effective and viable to perform its functions in the provision of social security benefits. This study seems to give support to Anthony Downs's (1967) position that the market-oriented organization tends to be efficient in the allocation of marketable benefits and divisible costs. Additionally, all three program areas investigated involve, to different extents, the delivery of "measurable outputs," in Robert Golembiewski's notion. According to Golembiewski's theory, the "product model" is more applicable than the "functional model" to the distribution of benefits and services in these three program areas to minimize supervision and procedural complexity, to install flat hierarchy and shorten communication lines, to employ simpler sets of evaluating criteria, to control deviation effectively, and thus to reduce work load and administrative cost (Golembiewski 1976). The benefits and services of all three program areas are basically excludable and for individual rather than joint use. Theoretically speaking, they can rely more heavily on the market mechanisms for their delivery and can thus bypass the problems of rigidity, complexity, and costs of the administrative hierarchy. By and large, since these three program areas concern tangible interests or "preferences" in Charles Lindblom's conceptual scheme, the "strategic model" of decision making is found more effective than the "synoptic model" in their provision, and "interaction" can substitute for abstract theory as a guide in the decision-making process (Lindblom 1977). All these theoretical perspectives suggest the diminishing role of state intervention in the policy areas of social security in China.

On the other hand, this chapter suggests, above all, that in spite of its reduced role, the state apparatus has some useful roles to play in the arena of social security in the PRC—for instance—in the provision of retirement benefits. As indicated in the preceding analysis, the centralization of the managerial power of retirement funds has taken place from the enterprise level to the state level (the local government level) in order to remedy the problems arising from the *ad hoc* arrangements of the enterprise-centered retirement system left by the cultural revolution. It is apparent, moreover, that the state hierarchy would still enjoy advantages in terms of its continuity, stability, and the needed scale for pooling resources and sharing risks. Closer to the synoptic model than to the strategic model, the state apparatus is appropriate for handling the substantive principles of state administration—such as income maintenance, security for the aged, and distributive justice—entailed in the income transfer between generations.

To sum up, services and benefits in all three program areas examined could functionally be transferred from the public sector to private sector in light of Downs's (1967) concepts of "marketable benefits" and "divisible costs," the Ostroms's (1977) criteria of "individual use" and "excludability" and Golembiewski's (1976) construct of "measurable output." However, these managerial concerns just noted are only necessary, but not sufficient, conditions for the progress of the "privatization movement" in the People's Republic of China. In the foreseeable future, such a privatization movement appears to be dictated by the restructuring of China's economic system, and ultimately by the economic growth and productivity of the society.

NOTES

The author wishes to register his appreciation to the John K. Fairbank Center for East Asian Research, the Coolidge Hall Library, and the Harvard-Yenching Library at Harvard University for providing facilities and assistance during 1990 to the research project on which this chapter is based.

1. With qualifications, authors have treated social security in China in a positive light as it is compared with that in other developing countries. For examples, see Ahmand and Hussain (1989).

2. For illustration, the expenditure for welfare and labor insurance (including medical care) remained in the region of 14–17 percent of the total wage bill from 1952 to 1978 (see Guojia 1983, 491). The percentage of capital construction investment funds allocated to urban housing was low and steady from 1953 to 1977 (see Kirby 1985).

3. One indication is a very impressive growth in spending for welfare and labor insurance (including medical care), increasing from 13.7 percent of the total wage bill in 1978 to 28.2 percent in 1988 (Guojia 1989, 151). There was also an increase in floor space for

urban residents from 4.2 square meters per person in 1978 to 8.8 square meters in 1988 (Guojia 1989, 756).

4. It is noteworthy that the discussions on the social security issues in the existing literature are a bit outdated in view of recently available material on the subject (see Cui 1988).

REFERENCES

Ahmand, Ehtisham, and Althar Hussain. 1989. *Social Security in China: A Historical Perspective.* Programme of Research into the Reform of Pricing and Market Structure in China STICERDO. London School of Economics.

Beijing xiehe yiyuan gaige lingdao xiaozhu. 1986. ''Sannian shidian gaige huigu yu fenxi'' (''Review and Analysis of the Pilot Programme of Reform for the Last Three Years''). *Zhong quo yiyuan guanli (Management of China's Hospitals)* 8:11–16.

Cai Derong. 1987. ''Zhongguo chengshi zhuzhai tizhi gaige yangjin'' (''A Study of the Urban Housing Reform in China''). Beijing: Zhonggue Caizheng jingji chubanshe.

''Chengshi siyou fangwu guanli tiaoli'' (''The Regulations Concerning the Management of Private Houses in Cities''). 1983. *Zhonghua renmin gongheguo guowuyuan gongbao* (hereafter referred to as *Guowuyuan gongbao*) (*Bulletin of the State Council*) 24:1157–60.

''Chengxiang jianche huanjing bachubu guanyu kuoda chengshi gongyou zhuzhai butian chushou shidian baogao'' (''The Report of the Ministry of Urban and Rural Environmental Protection on the Pilot Programme of the Subsidized Sale of Public Housing Units in Cities''). 1984. *Guowuyuan gongbao* (Bulletin of the state council), 18:921–24.

Chen Mingzheng. 1989. ''Zai quanguo weisheng tingjuzhang huiyishang de zhongjie jianghua'' (''The Concluding Speech to the National Conference of Chiefs of the Bureau Offices of Health Care''). *Zhongguo nongcun weisheng shiye guanli (Management of the Health Care in Rural China)* 3:1–13.

Cong Shuhai. 1986. ''Woguo zhigong yanglao baozhang zhidu xintan'' (''A Fresh Exploration on the Retirement System of Workers and Staff in Our Country''). *Caimou jingii (Economics of Finance and Trade)* 6:48–51.

Cui Naifu (Minister of Civil Administration). 1988. ''Tansuo you zhongguo teshe de shehui baozhang zhidu'' (''In Search of a Social Security System with Chinese Characteristics''). *Shehui baozhang bao (Social Security Daily)*, April 1, p. 3.

Davis, Deborah. 1988. ''Unequal Chances, Unequal Outcomes: Pension Reform and Urban Inequality.'' *China Quarterly* 114:223–42.

''Deng Xiaoping tongzhi guanyu jianzhuya he shuzhai wenti de tanhua'' (''Comrade Deng Xiaoping's Talk on the Construction Industry and Housing Problem''). 1984. *Xinhua yuebao (New China Monthly)* 5:115. (Originally published in *People's Daily*, May 15, 1984.)

Ding Yongfang. 1988. ''Qianyi shehui laodang bao-xian jijin de baozhi he zhengzhi'' (''Preliminary Analysis of the Maintenance and Appreciation of the Values of Labor Insurance Fund''). *Jingji Chan kao (Economic References)*, May 18, p. 4.

Downs, Anthony. 1967. *Inside Bureaucracy.* New York: Little Brown.

Du Chuanli, Xie Dong-liang, and He Hong-xuan. 1985. ''Quanmin suoyouzhi yiyuan tizhi gaige de shexiang'' (''Ideas for the Reform of the State-Owned Hospitals''). *Jingji tizhi gaige (Economic Reform)* 3:3.

50   Public Policy in China

Du Lexun. 1989. "Weisheng gaige yu fazhan de jige lilum yu shengee" ("Theory and Policy of the Development of the Healthcare"). *Zhong guo weisheng jingji (Economics of Health Care in China)* 2:32–35.

Feng Huijuan. 1986. "Woguo tuixiu zhigong duiwu de bianhua he tuixiu zhidu de yange" ("The Changing Composition of Pensioners in Our Country and the Evolution of the Retirement System"). *Zhongguo laodong kexue (China's Science of Labor)* 9:25.

Fu Huazhong. 1987. "Guaanyu Zhigong tuixiu teiyong shehui tongchou de wenti" ("The Problem of Unified Management of the Pension Fund for Workers and Staff at the Societal Level"). *Zhongguo laodong kexue (China's Science of Labor)* 6:9–11.

Gao Zhenrong. 1988. "Lui shehui bao-zhang shouru laiyuan de chongxin xuanzhe" ("The reselection of the Financial Sources of Social Security"). *Shehui baozhang bao (Social Security Daily)*, February 12, p. 3.

Golembiewski, Robert T. 1976. "Civil Service and Managing Work." In Robert T. Golembiewski et al., eds., *Public Administration*, 265–92. Chicago: Rand McNally College Publishing Company.

"Guanyu weisheng Gongzuo gaige ruogan zhengoe wenti de baogao" ("Report of the Reform Policies of the Health Service"). *Zhong quo yiyuan guanli (Management of China's Hospitals)* 8:5–7.

Guojia Tongjichu. 1989. *Zhongguo Tongji nianjian 1989 (China's Statistics Yearbook 1989)*. Hong Kong: Xiankong jianji daobao.

———. 1983. *Zhongguo Tongli Nianjian 1983. (China's Statistics Yearbook 1983)*. Hong Kong: Xiankong jianji daobao.

"Guowuyuan bangongting zhuanfa jiaaoyubu chengxiang jianshe huanjing baobubu quanguo jiaoyu gonghui guanyu quanguo gaishan chengshi zhongxiao-sue jiaozhiyuan tiaojian jingyan jiaoliuhui qingkuang the baogao de tongzhi" ("The Circular of the Report on the Conference of Exchange of Experience on the Improvement of Housing Condition of the Middle and Primary School Teachers by the Ministry of Education, the Ministry of Urban and Rural Environmental Protection, All China Federation of Teachers' Union as Transmitted by the Staff Office of the State Council"). *Guowuyuan Gongbao (Bulletin of the State Council)* 1:28–31.

"Guowuyuan guanyu tongyi yantaishi chengzhen zhufang zhidu gaige chixing fangan gei shandong renming zhengfu de pifu" ("The State Council's Consent on the Proposal for Trial Implementation of the Urban Housing Reform of Yendai Municipality in Its Reply to the People's Government of Shandong Province"). 1988. *Guowuyuan gongbao (Bulletin of the State Council)* 42–57.

"Guowuyuan guanyu yange kongzhi chengzhen zhuhai biaozhun de guiding" ("The Regulations of the State Council on the Strict Control over the Urban Housing Standards"). 1983. *Guowuyuan gongbao (Bulletin of the State Council)* 86:1156–57.

"Guowuyuan zhufang zhidu gaige lingdao xiaozhu 'guanyu zei guanguo chengzhen fengi fenqi tuixing zhufang zhidu gaige de shishi fang an," ("The Draft-Proposal for the Implementation of Housing Reform in Phases in Urban China"). 1988. *Xinhua yuebao (New China Monthly)* 3:88–91.

Huang Xiaojing and Yang Xiao. 1987. "From Iron Ricebowls to Labor Market: Reforming the Social Security System." In Bruce L. Reynolds, ed., *Reform in China*, 147–60. New York: M. E. Sharpe.

Hu Shanlian. 1989. "Zhongguo weisheng shiye guanli yanjin de sian zhuang" ("The Current Situation of the Management Study of China's Health Care"). *Zhongguo nongcun weisheng shiye guanli (Management of the Health Care in Rural China)* 3:21.

"Jainshe juyou zhongguo teshe de shehui bao-zhang zhidu" ("To Build a Social Security System with Chinese Characteristics"). 1989. *Lilun Xinni bao (Bulletin of Theories)*, Beijing, July 6. (Cited in *Laodong jingji yu renshi quanli [Economics of Labor and Personnel Management].*)

Kirby, R.J.R. 1985. *Urbanization in China: Town and Country in a Developing Economy, 1949-2000 AD.* London and Sydney: Croom Helm.

Ma, Laurence J. C. 1981. "Urban Housing Supply in the People's Republic of China." In Laurence J. C. Ma and Eduard W. Hantem, eds., *Urban Development in Modern China* 222-33. Boulder, Colo.: Westview Press.

Lee, Peter N. S., and Irene H. S. Chow. 1987. "The Remunerative System in State-Owned Industrial Enterprises in Post-Mao China: Changes and Continuity, 1979-1984." In Joseph C. H. Chai and Chi-Keung Leung, eds., *China's Economic Reform*, 181. Hong Kong: Center of Asian Studies, University of Hong Kong.

Lee, Yok-shiu F. 1988. "The Urban Housing Problem in China." *China Quarterly* 4:387-404.

Lindblom, Charles E. 1977. *Politics and Markets, the World's Political System.* New York: Basic Books.

Li Quanzhou. 1985. "Yiyuan jingji tizhi gaige de jige lilun wenti" ("Several Theoretical Problems of the Economic Reforms of the Hospital"). *Weisheng jingji (Economics of Health Care)* 8:3-7.

Liu Lili. 1987. "Jingji tizhi gaige xuyao shehui baozhang zhidu xiang peitao" ("Social Security System Should Be Synchronized with Economic Reform"). *Zhongguo jingji tizhi gaige (China's Economic Reform)* 1:189.

Liu Youjin. 1988. "Shilun zhufang xiaofei jijin zhubu naru zhigong gongzi jijin wenti" ("On the Problem of How to Incorporate Housing Fund into Wage Fund of Workers and Staff"). *Zhongguo laodong kexue (China's Science of Labor)* 5:29.

Ostrom, Vincent and Elinor. 1977. "Public Goods and Public Choices." In E. S. Savas, ed., *Alternatives for Delivering Public Services*, 7-14. Boulder, Colo.: Westview.

People's University of China. 1987. Xeroxed newspaper material. F102, No. 7:39-40.

Qiu Shanqi and Shi Mingcai. 1985. "Wo guo shehui baoxian de fazhan gaikuang" ("A Survey of the Development of Social Security in China"). *Zhongguo Laodong (China's Labor)* 12:23-26.

"Renzhen quanche jiuzheng jianfanz fenzfan buzheng shefen gongkai xin, zhongji yaoqiu sianqu jieshou he duke gongzhuo" ("The Open Letter Concerning the Rectification of the Improper Work Style Demand for Completing the Task of Verification and Supplementary Work In Time"). *Renmin Ribao (People's Daily)* February 28, 1984, p. 1.

Shi Mingcai. 1988. "Woguo zhigong tuixiu zhidu gaige huigu he jin yibu gaige de shilu" ("Some Thoughts on the Retrospect and Prospect of the Reforms of the Retirement System of Workers and Staff in Our Country"). *Zhongguo laodong kexue (China's Science of Labor)* 12:11-14.

Shirk, Susan. 1985. "The Politics of Industrial Reform." In Elizabeth J. Perry and Christine Wong, eds., *The Political Economy of Reform in Post-Mao China*. Cambridge, Mass.: Council on East Asian Studies.

"Shixing jingji quanli yiyuan mianmao yixin" ("To Introduce Economic Management and to Change the Appearance of the Hospital"). *Guizhou ribao (Guizhou Daily)*, October 8, 1981, p. 3.

Sun Mingyang. 1986. "Chengshi zhigong zhufang zhidu ying yu gonzi zhidu tongbu gaige" ("The Reform of Urban Housing System of Workers and Staff Should Be

Synchronized with the Wage System"). *Jingji tizhi gaige (Economic Reform)* 2:71–72.

Su Xing. 1987. "Woguo chengshi zhuzhai wenti" ("The Urban Housing Problem in China"). Beijing: Zhongguo shehui kexue chubanshe, 7–8.

Tong Yuanshi and Qian Shiming. 1985. "Zhigong ful fanchou tansuo he zhigong fuli zhido gaige" ("An Analysis of the Scope and Reform of Welfare of Workers and Staff"). *Shehui kexue (Social Sciences)* 1:15–19.

———. 1984. "Quanyu shehuizhuyi laodong baoxian ruogan wenti de tansue" ("Investigation on Several Problems of Socialist Labor Insurance"). *Caijing Xanjiu (Financial and Economic Research)* 2:34–40.

Walder, Andrew G. 1986. *Communist Neo-Traditionalism: Work and Authority in Chinese Industry.* Berkeley: University of California Press.

Walder, Andrew G. 1987. "Wage Reform and the Web of Factory Interests." *China Quarterly* 109:23–41.

Wang Yongjun. 1986. "Woguo chengzhen zhuzhai wenti de zhangjie yuchulu" ("The Problem and Solution of the Urban Housing in China"). *Zhongyang caizheng jinrong xueyuan xuuebao (Journal of Central Finance and Monetary College)* 6:60.

White, Gordon. 1987. "The Politics of Economic Reform: Introduction of the Labour Contract System." *China Quarterly* 111:365–89.

———. 1983. "Socialist Planning and Industrial Management: Chinese Economic Reform in the Post-Mao Era." *Development and Change* 14:483–574.

Whyte, Martin King, and William L. Parish. 1984. *Urban Life in Contemporary China.* Chicago: University of Chicago Press.

Wong, T. T. 1989. "The Salary Structure, Allowances, and Benefits of Shanghai Electronics Factory." *China Quarterly* 117:135–55.

Wu Guoqing, Feng Huazhang, and Ni Nai-cheng. 1988. "Guanyu gaige xianxing yanglao baoxian zhidu de yixie shexiang" ("Ideas of the Reform of the Existing Retirement Pension System"). *Zhongguo laodong kexue (China's Science of Labor)* 3:29–30.

Yan Huizhong. 1985. "Lun yiyuan tizhi gaige" ("On the Reform of Hospital Structure"). *Zhong quo yiyuan guanli (Management of China's Hospitals)* 8:8–12.

Zhang Qiufang. 1986. "Zhuzhai shangpinhua shi woguo jingji tizhigaige de yixiang zong da shengce" ("The Commercialization of Housing Is One of the Most Important Policies of the Economic Reform"). *Beijing daxue xuebao (Journal of Peking University)* 6:24.

Zhuang Jing. 1986. "Weisheng gongzuo gaige shexiang." *Jiankangbao (Beijing) (Health Care Daily)*, November 4, p. 1.

Zhuang Qidong and Li Jianli. 1985. "Tantan zhigong tuixiu baozian zhidu" ("Some Discussion on the Retirement Insurance System of Workers and Staff"). *Renmin Ribao (People's Daily)*, September 6, p. 5.

CHAPTER 4

Health Care Administration in China

Sun Guangde

Sun Guangde reviews health care administration in the People's Republic of China. In 1949, health services were confronted with widespread disease and lack of medical staff and medication. Both public and private hospitals existed but were generally poorly equipped. It was initially decided that both state and private ownership had significant roles to play in the provision of health care. Yet, private hospitals were slowly turned into public hospitals, and individual medical practitioners were strongly urged to set up joint clinics. Using the model of rural agricultural cooperatives, health care stations emerged in a similar collective mode.

Sun describes the horizontal and vertical leadership exercised on hospitals. There is direct vertical leadership from the government and horizontal professional guidance to the practitioners on separate levels. Sun says that the health services accepted administrative leadership from government and vocational guidance from health administrative departments. This has, however, had the unhappy consequence of fragmenting public health services and has interfered with appropriate medical responsiveness. Once again, the personnel issue reappears with the absence of reward for excellence and the lack of penalty for malfeasance.

In 1978, reforms were undertaken, with fixed quotas established for assignment, beds, staff size, professional technical norms, and funds. Each division was to have an "average quota of excellence," with the goal of achieving standardization and routinization of all functions. A secondary goal was to achieve a multiple system with the state as major practitioner, providing multiple forms of health care.

The management system used in health care also derives from industrial systems aiming at standardization of activities. Similar to developed nations, outpatient services have rapidly expanded. Coordination has helped limit the waste of health service resources. Although there have been attempts to link productivity to income, this is more difficult within a health system because of the collaborative activity required. In some instances, medical institutions have been guilty of overutilization. As Professor Sun says, "In a nutshell, they concoct all sorts of means to extract people's wealth." This is a typical complaint about many large and complex health systems.

Yet, in comparative terms, perhaps overutilization is not necessarily bad. One might question the base of comparison. If the people had been underserved for many years, it may take a while to deal with long-term, undiagnosed problems. Sun suggests that China build onto the system incrementally while recognizing certain limits to economic benefits. She also cautions that there may be a diminution in quality in order to increase profits. As one begins to fill in the gaps of the past, she notes, one has to recognize that this heightens the appetite for greater change. The importance of motivation for workers, as well as an emphasis on spiritual forces and moral character, is critical in health care, for, in truth, the hospital is the perfect embodiment of the link between the spiritual and the physical. When Sun says that public administrators should overcome disorder and confusion she is not alone in expressing this hope. Ultimately, the emerging form of socialized medicine should strengthen the PRC by balancing the infinite needs of an emerging nation within the framework of fiscal constraints.

THE FORMATION OF THE HEALTH CARE SYSTEM IN CHINA

Health care is one of the most important parts of social and public administration. It is necessary to discuss the health care administration in the study of the public administration in China. In the early years after the founding of the People's Republic of China, the health care services were in the serious situation of shortage of medical staff and medical supplies. There were three types of medical establishments: private hospitals, public hospitals, and private practitioners. According to the 1949 statistics, there were 541,240 health care workers, 80 percent of whom ran private practices, and 84,625 beds in 3,676 health care institutions nationwide. The number of hospital beds per 1,000 population was 0.15, and 23 percent of the beds were scattered across the rural areas with the rate of only 0.05 bed per one thousand people (Ministry of Public Health, 1989). In spite of the poor equipment and technology at that time, the charges for medical treatments remained unreasonably high, so that ordinary people could not afford good health care.

After the establishment of the new government, the health care authority started to carry out a full range of restoration, adjustment, and reformation in all health care services. The policy adopted was to allow both public and private ownership of the health care services, with each type having its role to play in the national health care system as a whole. The government played an active leading role in guiding the private services, arranging for them to run properly by taking into account the requirements of the national health care system, including encouragement of the cooperation among the health care services, improvement of the medical technology, and gradual transformation of the private to the public.

To put this policy into effect, the government made it clear that each hospital or practitioner must take responsibility for local health care and the prevention of epidemic diseases. The government would assist in mobilizing the financial resources and in improving the administration in these private practices and also supply the new equipment and qualified medical professionals. The government imposed standards on medical charges to make sure that the private practices served the purpose of health care for the people. Unemployed medical workers were allowed to run their own practices, which were then combined into hospitals or clinics if the owner agreed to do so. These hospitals and clinics were of a collective nature that was not fully financed by the government.

During the first five-year plan (1953–1957), the above-mentioned private establishments were gradually transformed into public hospitals. In the meantime, a number of health care stations were set up by the agricultural cooperatives in the rural area. By 1956, the number of grass-roots health care centers in the countryside had increased to more than 74,000, with 64,000 owned by the cooperatives, accounting for 82 percent of that nation's total number of medical institutions. These efforts made by the new government led to the formation of a network able to carry out both medical treatment and disease prevention.

THE PROBLEM IN THE HEALTH CARE ADMINISTRATION BEFORE THE REFORM

The prereform health system played a positive role in national development by mobilizing work-force, material, and financial resources for the development of health care services, but its inherent deficiencies also generated some negative factors, which to some extent hampered the growth of the health care system in China.

One deficiency was an overlapped and separated health care administration. The central government and the local government—at provincial, municipal, and county levels—each had a subordinated public health department, which was responsible to its own superior; this department took professional direction rather than administrative instructions from the higher-level health department. For example, the county health department would be responsible to the county council and would take the professional guidance from the municipal or provincial health department. Therefore, it was impossible for the Ministry of Public Health of the central government to exercise direct administration over a lower-level health care unit unless through the local government, and there was no responsibility relationship between the higher-level and the lower-level health department except the professional instructions. As for the health departments at the same level, there was neither an administrative relation nor a business contact.

Although most of the health care institutions were under the jurisdiction of either the central government or the local governments, a fairly large portion of the institutions were attached to the industry, transport, and telecommunication ministries or were subordinated to the armed forces or higher education institutions; they responded only to their direct superior and served only the units within their own sectors. These attached health care institutions were expected to carry out the health policies, regulations, and technical criteria made by the government health ministry but were not responsible to it. In the daily routines, there was neither direct leadership nor professional guidance between them.

The above-mentioned deficiencies created a situation in which an overlapped and separated health care administration prevailed, with each health department or unit doing things in its own way and developing its own health care system. Thus, it was difficult to plan the future development of the national health care system as a whole. There had been numerous cases of overdevelopment and lack of planning, which brought about tremendous waste of work-force, material, and financial resources.

This system, which stressed administrative management, resulted in the overcentralization of the power in the central and local government branches and led to the lack of necessary rights in such aspects as personnel, finance, and material for the health care institutions and to excessive intervention from superior organs. This system gave no economic aspect of health care management. For a long time, the state has applied the "full amount reimbursement budget" within such health care organs as epidemic prevention management centers, and has practiced "supplementing the balance," namely subsidizing the difference between the actual revenues and the expenditures in other medical institutions. Therefore, health care organs were made to depend entirely on the state, and the performance of these organs, good or bad, gain or loss, had neither exerted pressure nor given incentives to officials and the staff. Officials of these health care organs seldom analyzed their own economic activities, busying themselves in hankering after manpower, money, and equipment from higher authorities, which in fact nurtured the inclination of "waiting, depending, and requesting." In the meantime, work performance had no effect on individuals or institutions—no rewards for excellent work and no punishments for poor performances. This proved detrimental to mobilizing enthusiasm, initiative, and creativeness in the health care services and staff. The economic effectiveness and economic responsibility were neglected in health care services, thereby seriously hampering their upgrading and development. As a result, after 1958, diversified ownerships of the health care services, with state-owned services as the main body, were turned into the unitary system of state ownership. Thus, not only was the financial burden of the state aggravated, with the number of health care networks decreased, but also the enthusiasm of health care workers was dampened and the development of the health services was hindered.

THE MAIN CONTENTS OF THE REFORM IN HEALTH CARE ADMINISTRATION

After 1979, reforms swept through health care services and other institutions in China. Aiming at the shortcomings and deficiencies mentioned above, the reform in health care services has chiefly been made in three areas.

First, the state began to implement a responsibility system in medical and health care institutions. The essence of this system is the "five fixed quotas," namely fixed assignment, fixed number of beds, fixed size of staff, fixed professional technical norms, and fixed quota of subsidiary funds. The amount of subsidy is determined mainly according to the actual situation of hospitals and their needs, with due consideration for the present ability of subsidization. The remainder between revenue and expenditure is used for medical equipment and employees' welfare. These reform measures expanded the autonomy of health care institutions at the grass-roots level, and played an important part in sparking the initiatives of health care institutions as well as employees in improving the social and economic benefits of health care services.

The responsibility system that is characterized by fixed quota management, quality control, assessment by different levels, and floating wage was implemented within the health care sector:

Fixed Quota Management: The fixed quotas are size of staff, assignment, indicators of cost and benefit, and so on. Setting up an advanced average quota for every job formulates the duties that should be fulfilled by various staff members. Meanwhile, working procedures and job responsibilities are established for those jobs that are not appropriate to be managed by fixed quotas. Therefore, everyone has a job, every job has its responsibilities, every part of each job has indicators. Fixed quota management is the basis of the implementation of the responsibility system, and is the fundamental criterion of assessment upon which rewards and punishment are decided.

Quality Control: This is control of all the possible factors that might influence the quality of health care services so as to achieve standardization, normalization, institutionalization, optimization, and digitalization in the process of health care technical management and make comparative analyses. It is conducted on the basis of fixed quota management. Meanwhile, setting up corresponding resource consumption indicators at every link of service is another step in realizing the combination of technical efficiency and economic benefit.

Assessment by Different Levels: The indicators of quantity, quality, costs, and economic effectiveness will be broken down to every department, every section, and every person, each being responsible to a superior. After the assessment indicators and methods are formulated, the progress in fulfillment of the above-mentioned indicators will be checked regularly.

Floating Wage: The distribution of income is closely hinged to performance of sections and individuals, with a well-defined employee-to-section and section-to-hospital relationship.

Second, the state began to reform the state monopoly in the health sector, in order to develop a diversified and multi-channel-financed health care system with the state as the main body. The unemployed medical professionals were allowed to run their private practices, which made the available health care human resources better utilized and accessed. Some qualified private practitioners got licenses to run their own practices after passing the examination sponsored by the health department in charge. According to the 1987 statistics, there are 139,708 private practitioners, about 3 percent of all the professionals (Ministry of Public Health 1989). Health care authorities also corrected the practice of exercising administration over collectively owned medical and health care institutions with the same methods as applied to state institutions and restored the management principles suitable to health care and medical institutions of a collective nature: independent accounting, assuming sole responsibility for profits or losses, to each according to his work, and democratic management. Under several prerequisites—strictly complying with standard medical charges stipulated by the state, fulfilling health care and prevention assignments, and guaranteeing quality—health care services may expand the scope of services, reasonably organize revenue, and cut down expenses. In case there is a surplus in the budget, health care services may draw a specified proportion for business development, collective welfare, and bonuses. The wages and welfare closely associate with the economic benefits of the unit itself while taking reference to the criteria of government employees and in conformity with the relevant regulations.

Third, the state began to develop medical cooperatives. This is a new form of medical organization emerged in the reform process of China's health care system so as to facilitate and benefit the people, to prevent and cure diseases, and to improve the health status. Its guiding principles are voluntary integration and mutual benefit while giving consideration to the interests of the state, the collective, and the individual. This approach frees health care services from regional and subordinating restrictions and brings about horizontal alliance. Before the establishment of the medical cooperatives, some key hospitals in middle and large cities had great advantages and potentialities in respect to their medical technology, personnel, and advanced medical facilities, yet they could not fully meet the demands of the society in such routine service as capacity of outpatient service, the number of hospital beds, and ordinary medical and nursing personnel as well as logistical service. On the other hand, there were quite a few hospitals with considerable scale, which were attached to the manufacturing and mining enterprises, and institutions of these cities. The routine service facilities of these attached hospitals —such as outpatient service, hospital beds, and ordinary medical personnel— possessed great potentialities. These hospitals had sufficient funds to install advanced medical equipment; however, due to a lack of senior technical professionals, they were unable to make full use of their potentialities. The establishment of medical and health care cooperatives enables senior professionals from central hospitals in cities to take regular on-duty service and treatment of the patients at hospitals attached to mining and manufacturing enterprises, ordinary hospitals, and community clinics of city districts. In this way, the technical professionals of big hospitals have a better opportunity to display their abilities, and the economic resources of those attached hospitals have a better chance to meet the needs of the society. In some cities, the outpatient service capacity and beds for hospitalization have rapidly expanded, tantamount to setting up several hospitals, each with hundreds of beds.

Medical cooperatives have greatly reduced the waste of health service resources caused by the practice of separating administration into various departments and regions. Even though still unable to resolve the problem completely, the cooperatives reflect the trend of socialization in the development of health care service, improving the efficiency of the utilization of health care resources as well as the technical level of health care services and quality of treatment.

REFORM OF HEALTH CARE ADMINISTRATION: REVIEW AND PROSPECT

Some of the approaches in health care reform mentioned above have not been pursued across the country and are still in the experimental stage. But these reforms have already achieved remarkable results.

First, the new administrative system closely linked the performance of the hospital and labor contribution with the rewards of medical personnel. The more work a person does, the more income he or she receives. It mobilized the working enthusiasm of hospital staff, thereby raising the efficiency to a great extent. The volume of service has remarkedly increased; it is easier to be hospitalized and be treated; the service attitude of the medical and health care staffs has improved immensely.

Second, the rate of equipment utilization has been greatly raised. Also, the waiting period of some items for medical examination has been shortened from one month to one week or two days, thus better satisfying the pressing needs of the patients.

Third, the new system has enhanced internal management and remarkably improved the hospital management. The reform has prompted the internal sections at different levels of the hospital to make all-around investigations and gather statistics about the funds and labor conditions. The hospitals have also established or amplified the system of statistics and reports and have extensively enhanced the accounting systems of the hospital itself, the divisions and sections, and the sick-area and various wards. The hospitals have made improvements on income distribution, working out various piece-rate wage systems and floating wage systems.

Fourth, the new management system has heightened the consciousness of the independent management and has made the hospitals more animated. Formerly, hospitals depended on the state for financial allocation; now they have to rely on the quality and quantity of the services they provide. Finally, the new system has increased revenues and granted hospitals a certain degree of right to manage independently. Hospitals may draw development funds from their profits to ameliorate the condition of their equipment. They may also appropriate encouragement funds to improve the financial conditions of their staffs.

In the process of reform, however, a number of problems have arisen: some medical institutions, in their pursuit of profits, gave some additional dosage of medicine on prescriptions so as to sell more; some X-ray departments deliberately took two pictures for two separate localities when only one picture for one locality was needed; one lab test may have been enough, yet the technician made two or more; and ultrasonic B detection was done even though it was not needed at all. In short, all sorts of excuses are concocted to make profits. Overdose prescriptions, unnecessary examinations, and unreasonable charging of fees have led to a sharp increase in expenditures by both the patients and the health care services, adding to the financial burden of free medicare and the labor insurance medicare.

The effects of the reform are obvious, and so are the problems. How shall we then evaluate the reform of the administrative system in health care services? One opinion insists that reforms in the administrative system are dubious and should even be negated, whereas another opinion argues that the orientation and principles of the reform are correct although it is neither mature nor perfect due to the lack of experience and relatively short period of implementation. Therefore, the reform should be consummated through continuing experiments instead of giving up halfway. Taking heed of experiences and lessons from previous reforms, we should pay more attention to the following issues.

First, the reform can stimulate everything but cannot replace everything. The basic requirements of the economic reform are to establish correct relations among three parties—the state, the enterprise, and the individual—through adjusting the relationship among them. All these measures could liberate the enterprises from unnecessary fetters, encouraging the enthusiasm, initiative, and creativeness of the individuals and heightening the vitality and vigor of the enterprises. Therefore, the reform possesses the power to promote work and provide impetus to the comprehensive work. Nonetheless, the reform cannot solve all problems in management, even though it may accelerate the solution to specific problems. It is unreasonable to expect that once the institutional reform is staged, all the problems in other aspects will be resolved readily. Therefore, while carrying out the administrative reform in health care services, we must at the same time rationalize specific management work. Without the cooperation of specific management work and the coordination of various aspects, administrative reform in health care services will evoke negative results.

Second, the incentive function of economic interests is not omnipotent but has its limits. Before the economic system reform, health care services were subsidized by the state, and hospitals did not have to shoulder any economic responsibility. The reform has made the hospitals assume a certain degree of economic responsibility: revenues are linked with the performance; the income of the staff is related to work quality; and economic benefits have become a factor that pushes hospital business forward. Nevertheless, we should be aware that economic benefits sometimes cause a health care unit and its staff, in the interest of their own profits, to provide overcharged services with lower quality, which is harmful to the interest of the people. Also, the needs of humankind are many, and although material needs are the basic ones they are not the sole ones. Besides material needs, people have spiritual needs, and their enthusiasm cannot be fully sparked with material benefits alone. During a specific period of time, material benefits are fairly restricted. Yet the average person's desire for material benefits is gradually growing. If society depends entirely on material benefits to stimulate people's initiatives, negative factors will ensue. In any society at any time, whatever the social system is, there are certain spheres in which material benefits do not work. On such occasions, we have to rely on spiritual force, on lofty ideology, on noble sentiments and moral characters. The hospital, being a place where the wounded are healed and the dying are rescued, needs spiritual force to surmount the economic benefits. In short, it cannot do without the stimulation of economic benefits, but depending excessively or entirely on economic benefits will not work either.

Third, the economic activities of the hospitals resemble the activities of the enterprises but still have their own peculiarities. Therefore, it is essential on the one hand to implement the general principles of economic reform while, on the other hand, taking special measures in the administrative reform of health care services. The economic system reform in China is aimed at the malpractices existing in the highly centralized economic administrative system. And naturally, its first step is to transfer responsibility, power, and profits to enterprises, which may be properly termed as "the state devoluting power to and sharing profits with the enterprises." The revenues of the enterprises and the personal income of the workers should be hooked up with economic benefits, thus mobilizing the vitality and vigor within the enterprises. Hospitals, though different from enterprises, are not profit-yielding establishments. Then from where do the profits come to stimulate the enthusiasm of the hospitals? They can only come from outside the hospital: either the state increases the financial subsidies to hospitals in a planned way, or the hospitals schematically raise charges to a reasonable level. Without consciously and schematically adopting these two measures and taking due consideration of the characteristics of the hospital, the hospital and its staff will increase income by shifting the burden to the patients. This is the crux of the matter: while implementing the general principles of the reform, the hospital must consider them in light of its own characteristics and take corresponding specific measures.

In further carrying out the reform, we should solve three problems. First, simultaneously with strengthening the vitality and vigor within the health care institution, we must also establish restraining mechanisms in society and institution itself. Second, while developing medical coordinating cooperatives through mobilizing social forces from all walks of life and by putting into practice the multichannel, multiform approach to include the state, the collective, and the individual to promote health care services, we should also enhance macro-management and control and perfectly planned administration and eliminate the phenomenon of "disorder and confusion." Third, we must amplify and strengthen the responsibility system of comprehensive target administration. The system reform should bring along the enhancement and perfection of other aspects: technical administration, economic management, administration management, and ideological education. At present, health care services and various other units are summing up the experiences and lessons of the previous phase of the reform, continuing to enhance the measures and rules and regulations of the reform, and exploring the road ahead of us.

No matter what future developments will unfold before our eyes, the following trends are inexorable. First, the development of medical and health care services will transit from government-invested and -initiated to multiformed, multichannel investment by the state, the collective, and the individual. Second, financial compensation to health care services will go through the transitional stage from depending entirely on government financial subsidy to being reasonably borne by the three parties: the state, the collective, and the individual. Third, the reform will amplify the economic management of the health care establishment, implement economic accounting, adhere to the prerequisite that social benefits are of prime importance, raise the economic benefits, and implement the principles of material profits. Finally, the system reform will continue to develop different forms of coordinating cooperatives, shifting from overlapped administration to the unified socialized administration.

REFERENCES

Cao Peiwen. 1987. "Restructuring the Management Patterns of the Health Care System in China." Presentations at the Third Annual Conference of the Chinese Society of Health Economics, Beijing.

Chang Ying. 1987. "Medical Ethics and Health Service Reform." *Chinese Health Economics* (a journal of the Chinese Society of Health Economics, Beijing) (August), SN54.

Du Lexun. 1990. "Reform of Health Service and Renewal of Ideas." *Chinese Health Economics* (January), SN83.

Ministry of Health, People's Republic of China. 1989. Statistics.

Sun Guangde. 1990. "The Nature, Level, and Fund Sources of Welfare." *Chinese Health Economics* (January), SN83.

———. 1987. "Internal Contradictions and Its Solution Approaches of Medical and Health Care." Presentations at the Third Annual Conference of the Chinese Society of Health Economics, Beijing.

Wang Bin. 1987. "On the Rise and Use of Funds of Health Service in Our Country." *Chinese Health Economics* (July), SN53.

Wu Xiang. 1988. "Hospital Ownership Should Be Properly Separated from Managerial Authority." *Chinese Health Economics* (January), SN59.

Xie Youxue. 1988. "Several Issues about the Reform of Labour Prevention and Medicare System in State-Owned Enterprises." *Labour Science of China* (November). Beijing.

Ye Yurong. 1990. "Increase Vigour of Health Service Units with the Aid of Market Mechanism." *Chinese Health Economics* (January), SN83.

CHAPTER 5

Environmental Control in the PRC

Hon S. Chan, K. C. Cheung, and Jack M. K. Lo

In the discussion of environmental control, Hon S. Chan, K. C. Cheung, and Jack M. K. Lo discuss the role of the government since 1972. Similar to the United States, China has experienced difficulties in selective enforcement and underenforcement.

The Environmental Protection Committee of the State Council was established in 1974 with the idea of coordinating environmental management within the various units of government. One of the first important tasks was to detect environmental pollution and then, second, to find ways to enforce such policies without necessarily hindering economic development and growth. This chapter concentrates specifically on the City Environmental Implementation Unit within Guangzhou. This particular unit is responsible for setting up the proper environmental controls and establishing the proper new technology.

The Law of Environmental Protection emphasizes the responsibility of local administrations to set up the appropriate laws and regulations on the basis of their own level of economic development and the nature of their pollution problems. There is great variation within the standards imposed, as well as the fines levied. Probably with an eye to efficiency and feasibility, the local authorities have extensive powers to deal with waste gas, waste water, and waste residue.

The national strategy emphasizes prevention. Within Guangzhou, before any construction can be undertaken, environmental impact assessments must be completed. Pollution fines are determined so as to guide future performance and also to pay for the cost of pollution control. In many instances within Guangzhou, there are great differences in opinion between those who are pro-growth and those who are pro-environment. It is ultimately up to the state to balance these conflicting needs. There is an effort within Guangzhou to further refine its mechanisms of monitoring the control of waste water. Level of concentration is one factor, but the total volume of waste water is also a well-regulated aspect.

On the matter of fines, levying penalties generates funds that will provide revenue to help enterprises undertake technical reform. Guangzhou, the equivalent of an American enterprise zone, considers the need for economic development as being superior to that of environmental control. Nonetheless, it recognizes the need for both activities to take place concurrently. The economic growth of Guangzhou permits support for environmental management. The authors provide detailed material regarding investments and activities. They assert that the policy outcomes result from power struggles. When resources are no longer centralized, the power conflict establishes new forms. As the structure becomes more formalized, the result is more informal accommodations and perhaps less feasible techniques for problem resolution.

Their analysis of the environmental problems within a growing and largely well-treated area is important to future development. Inasmuch as the policies are only now being applied, some time must be left for the assessment of their impact, for this can have serious consequences for the future development of other enterprise zones within China. The authors note that policy can be formulated by governmental as well as nongovernmental units in the interest of building a stronger substructure. Organizational dynamics and class relationships also contribute to some problems in which differences in status and rank limit the authority of individuals to request modifications. Thus, there tends to be more bargaining with environmental management than could have been anticipated.

There is no supreme acceptance of what the environmental managers want, but there is, as is perhaps natural within many structures, a tendency to try to negotiate more favorable circumstances. There appears to be a standoff when power is dispersed socially in such a way that no single unit of government is sufficiently powerful to force the others to conform. Although there is still a separate identity between the party and the state, the most effective policy implementation is prevented. The authors predict that as economic development becomes even more developed, there will be attendant difficulties in dealing with the pollution problem. The problems that the authors refer to deal with pollution design within a larger environmental setting. They suggest that attention must be paid to organizational hierarchy changes, as well as to integrating the resources and power of those outside the official government units.

Environmental degradation is a reality facing too many nations in the world. Regardless of differences in ideologies, political structures, and social and economic developments, it is expected that the government will assume a greater and active role in environmental control. Only since China took part in the Stockholm Conference on Human Environment in 1972 has the country viewed environmental management as vital. In 1973, China held its first national conference on environmental protection. After more than two decades of deliberation and preparations,

China promulgated its "Law of Environmental Protection" and a series of other related decrees in 1989. All agencies responsible for environmental control were then given a legal and legitimate status, with the hope that they would possess greater enforcing powers.

In all organizations and polities, there is always a disjunction between leadership intention, organizational behavior, and the actual results of an action. At the field level in China, underenforcement and selective enforcement of environmental control are two major problems. One basic task confronting the public-policy analysts is to describe and explain the state's steering mechanism and the external forces that contend with the entire government in the course of policy implementation. The difficulty of obtaining compliance when policy is to be implemented does not rest merely on factors such as policy design and resource support. On the basis of in-depth interviews with the management staff at different levels in the Guangzhou Environmental Protection Office and the Guangzhou Monitoring Station (in the following discussion, these two offices will be jointly referred to as the "Guangzhou environmental management"), we believe that the policy-implementation problems derive also from the relationship between policy and the environmental settings. Modern policy analysis attempts to provide a generic framework in explaining the implementation problem in China.

The chapter will first review the management structure, the management ethos, and the major measures undertaken for environmental control in Guangzhou. It will then examine the various advantages and drawbacks in using the prevailing models of decision making, accounting for policy-implementation problems in China. The authors will attempt to develop a conceptual framework and to outline the range of relevant factors that must be considered for any major implementation study to be undertaken in China.

THE MANAGEMENT STRUCTURE IN GUANGZHOU ENVIRONMENTAL CONTROL

Guangzhou is an important political, economic, cultural, and transportation center in the southeastern region of China. The total area of the city is 7,434.6 square kilometers, with a population of 5.854 million. It is one of the fourteen coastal open ports. Guangzhou has long been an industrial bastion of southern China, with diverse industry. Light industries are especially well developed. With the unfolding of economic reform since 1978, the city has striven to uphold the principles of "proper balance between economic, social and environmental benefits" and "the insistence on the synchronous planning, implementation and development of economic, city and environmental constructions" (Gan, Chan, and Wu 1990, 1).

In 1974, the State Council established the leading group of Environmental Protection and its office in charge of the country's work on environmental protection. In 1982, the Ministry of Urban and Rural Construction and Environmental Protection was created. In 1984, the ministry was put under the direct supervision of the State Council, thus extending its authority and scope of powers. In the same year, a new organization, the Environmental Protection Committee of the State Council, was set up to coordinate the environmental management of different provinces, prefectures, cities, and counties in the country. Since then, the provinces, prefectures, cities, and most of the counties have also set up individual environmental protection committees.

In Guangzhou City, the mayor heads the City Environmental Protection Committee (CEPC) and its office. Its main task is to make important decisions and solve the arising dilemmas concerning environmental protection. Practically speaking, the committee provides a chance for all agencies involved in environmental control to exchange information and feedback, to obtain financial and personnel support, and to negotiate.

Figure 5.1 shows the environmental management structure in Guangzhou. Some important observations can be made. First, a society-wide control network in detecting environmental pollution has been effectively created. The city government, through county and regional bureaus, gives district and governmental offices at various levels corresponding powers to report and monitor pollution control. Second, there are more than twenty agencies for the committee to coordinate. Thus, the management structure has created tremendous coordination and administrative problems. The City Planning, the City Economic Development, and the City Industrial-Commercial offices, for instance, are very reluctant to enforce stringent environmental policies, since these policies may hinder economic development and growth.

Figure 5.2 illustrates the City Environmental Protection Implementation Units. The most important unit is the Guangzhou Environmental Monitoring Station (GEMS), which directs environmental control. This unit oversees the work of different county, regional, district, and street monitoring stations. In collaboration with the City Research Institute for Environmental Science and the City Environmental Equipment Company, this office designs, develops, and helps manufacture environmental equipment and helps supply new technology to the various low-level monitoring stations. This office undertakes all essential environmental control tasks, such as collecting and evaluating the environmental-impact analysis submitted by both "private" and "public" units and undertaking regular as well as irregular site inspections. The GEMS works directly with the office of the CEPC, the highest policy-making body in Guangzhou's environmental control. Essentially, the GEMS is hierarchically responsible to the office of the CEPC.

To obtain a full picture of how environmental management operates in Guangzhou, it is necessary to understand the relationship between the national administration in Beijing and the regional office of the CEPC in Guangzhou. It would be incorrect to assume that the National Ministry of Environmental Protection in Beijing exercises a close supervision over the office of the CEPC in Guangzhou. The *Law of Environmental Protection* (Draft) in 1979 clearly stated that local administrations responsible for environmental management in different provinces, prefectures, cities, counties, and districts should come up with their

Figure 5.1
Environmental Management Structure in Guangzhou City

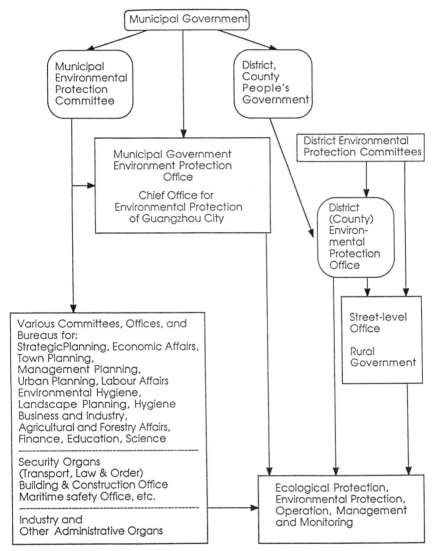

Source: Office of Environmental Protection, Guangzhou City.

Figure 5.2
City Environmental Protection Implementation Units

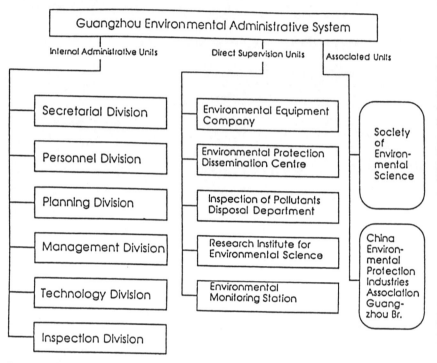

Source: Office of Environmental Protection, Guangzhou City

own corresponding laws and regulations on the basis of the level of economic development and the nature of their pollution problems (*Law of Environmental Protection*, Draft, 1979; Wong 1990). Consequently, different places in China have different standards and requirements in levying fees for the discharge of contaminants. Three of the highest officials in the office of the City Environmental Protection Committee and three in the City Environmental Monitoring Station reiterated this fact with respect to Guangzhou. Qu Geping, Director General of the National Ministry of Environmental Protection, explained to the third National Environmental Protection Committee in 1989 that the national environmental protection policy gives local authorities extensive and appropriate powers, reflecting the previously mentioned regional factors. Qu reiterated that the role of the National Ministry is to set up the national standards and the general national policies in environmental control (Qu 1989). Pointedly, in examining the zoning of decision-making authority in China's environmental control, we can characterize the relationship between the National Ministry of Environmental Control and the Guangzhou environmental management as "decentralized."

Two examples can best illustrate the point. First, the national "three wastes policy" delegates to the local environmental monitoring stations the power to quantify the environmental planning indices for managing the factory's "three wastes," that is, waste gas, waste water, and waste residue. The Guangzhou Environmental Monitoring Station, in consultation with the Office of the City Environmental Protection Committee, can set up the environmental protection planning indices over time depending on the contingent economic and social needs in Guangzhou. These include the following: (1) the annual "three wastes" and noise pollution management projects; (2) the treatment rate, the treatment capacity of the new waste water, waste gas, and waste residue, and the removal quantity of the major pollutants of the year; (3) the management of the major polluting constructions; and (4) the moving and rectification plan for heavy polluting factories. The planning indices are assigned to the polluting industries and units in the form of a project responsibility contract system.

Second, under the national strategy of "prevention better than controlling environmental problem" (Wong 1990, 3; Qu and Jin 1984, 10), the National Ministry had developed the "three simultaneous points" policy. In line with the *Law of Environmental Protection*, the Municipal Environmental Protection Office had promulgated the "Execution Measures for Controlling New Pollution from Generating." In accordance with these measures, before any building, expanding, or rebuilding constructions can actually be undertaken, an environmental-impact assessment must be completed. Also, it is stated that pollution-prevention mechanisms and the principal parts of a project must be designed, constructed, and put into production simultaneously. The local authorities need to decide on the selection of sites for construction projects depending on the ecological and environmental impacts of the projects. The local authorities must put forward the requirements for controlling the categories, concentration, and volume of the pollutants' discharge generated from the construction projects (Gan, Chan, and Wu 1990, 3–4).

Examining the relationship between the National Ministry of Environmental Protection and the Guangzhou Environmental Management from the viewpoint of financial resource seems to further reinforce the viewpoint that there is a "fragmented" relationship. Before 1984, the Guangzhou environmental management derived its financial support from the national administration and municipal government. After 1984, under the national strategy of "polluters bearing the cost generated," the Guangzhou Environmental Monitoring Station imposed a "pollution fine" for the discharge of pollutants. Fines are mainly directed against those who have caused severe pollution and, in consequence, damaged the economy and public health. For serious cases, in addition to a fine, an "economic court" is held to investigate the offender's legal responsibilities (Qu and Jin 1984, 17).

The actual amount of the pollution fine is determined by the local authorities and, in principle, is higher than the cost of pollution control. A higher fine is levied because 80 percent of the fines are rebated to the polluting units to raise funds for the purpose of updating technological processes and eliminating the "three wastes" in the course of production. The remaining 20 percent of the pollution fines are kept by the local environmental management to cover administrative costs, the expenses of research and development on basic theories and applied sciences such as environmental chemistry, biology, acoustics, and atmospheric environment, and the costs of developing renewable energy such as hydroelectric power and biogas. Apart from fulfilling the policy intent of "polluters bearing the cost generated," all the senior officials being interviewed in the office of the City Environmental Protection Committee and the Environmental Monitoring Station suggested that the "pollution fine" measure is employed to achieve "financial independence."

In 1983, before this measure was adopted, environmental management in Guangzhou received around four to five million yuan from the national administration and the municipal government. The amount certainly did not adequately cover all the expenses. The environmental management group had to apply for supplementary appropriations from the National Ministry of Environmental Protection. In doing so, the environmental management in Guangzhou was subject to close budgetary and policy scrutiny from the national administration. In 1989, the environmental management in Guangzhou obtained forty million yuan from the employment of the "pollution fine" policy (Chan et al. 1990).

Evidence shows that the environmental management in Guangzhou maintains a high level of "financial independence" from the national administration. "Financial self-sufficiency" guarantees less-frequent intervention from the national administration in Beijing. The findings provide a preliminary indication that in the zoning of decision-making authority and of financial-resource management, the Guangzhou environmental management has considerable autonomy.

THE MANAGEMENT ETHOS IN GUANGZHOU ENVIRONMENTAL CONTROL

Regardless of rank and seniority, all the interviewees—amounting to 10 percent of the staff in the two offices—expressed a strong consensus on the need to maintain a high level of economic development and growth. This view raises some questions about how the officials define their role and whether their attitude is one of pro-growth or pro-environment. Generally speaking, the higher the level of economic development, the higher the level of environmental pollution (see figure 5.3 for illustration).

The senior officials argued that the needs of development and environmental control are interdependent. The lower officials, with less than five years' working experience, reiterated the need for development, although some admitted that rapid economic growth could cause uninvited environmental problems. It is interesting to see how the operation of the environmental management in China in general and in Guangzhou in particular supports the interdependence of economic development and environmental control.

Figure 5.3
Economic Development and Environmental Quality, Guangzhou City, 1980–88

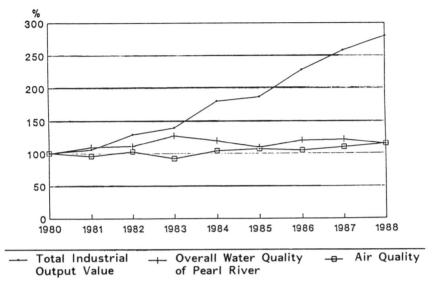

Source: Guangzhou Environmental Monitoring Station.

As previously mentioned, Article 4 of the *Law of Environmental Protection*, 1989, shows that the need of the national economic and social development plan is perceived as having the same legal status as the need of environmental protection. In illuminating how the state can integrate environmental protection with a national economic and social development plan, Qu Geping explained in the *People's Daily* on May 9, 1990 that environmental protection must evolve from and build on the national economic and social development (Qu 1990). Accordingly, in the course of designing the national economic and social development plan, the state must balance the need of maintaining economic and social development, population control, and resource management with the need for environmental protection. There is no indication that the need for environmental protection must outweigh, for instance, the need for economic development and growth.

On another occasion, Qu, in summarizing China's experience in environmental protection, said: "We are in favor of economic development and protecting and improving the environment within this development. We do not agree with the pessimistic view which calls for stopping or slowing down the tempo of economic development so as to protect and improve the environment" (Qu and Jin 1984, 7). He further stated that environmental protection was tantamount and complementary to the protection of social productivity and that practice proved that the prevention and control of environmental degradation was conducive to the promotion and maintenance of development (Qu and Jin 1984, 19; Qu 1989). Seen in this light, economic development has no less an important policy priority than environmental protection.

At the field level, the senior- and middle-rank officials in Guangzhou's two offices strongly supported the need for sustaining economic development. Working under the parameter set forth by the national administration, the Guangzhou environmental management needs to formulate policies in line with Guangzhou's economic development. Flexible and incremental policy programs must be created to accommodate the needs of environmental control and economic development and growth. Policy programs must fit into the demographic and geographic uniqueness in Guangzhou. To put into action such a policy intent, the Guangzhou environmental management must consider the nature and extent of pollution to be tolerated in the short run and must come up with the quantifiable yet flexible indices to implement the policy. These measures would not hinder economic growth. They would also be incremental measures to effectively control the spreading and deterioration of pollution problems. Over time, the quantified indices would be amended and more stringent measures introduced and enforced. The control of waste water, for example, is now measured by analyzing the level of concentration of the pollutant. This is the measure of "absolute concentration analysis." The Guangzhou environmental management will soon amend this measure and introduce the "total volume analysis." According to this new measure, not only the level of concentration but also the total volume of waste water to be discharged will be regulated (Gan, Chan, and Wu 1990, 8).

The middle- and lower-rank officials genuinely believed that without prosperous economic growth, technical reform would not be possible. For instance, the dyeing industries can now install high-temperature and high-pressure devices. In the past, without adequate financial and technical support, these industries could rely only on low-temperature and low-pressure machines, which were highly energy consuming and polluting. As street-level bureaucrats, these officials believed that the technical reform of old enterprises should center on achieving high economic benefits, improving the technological level, developing "major" products, saving energy and resources, and reforming commodity structures. From 1981 to 1987, the total investment in technological updating by all nationalized enterprises was 70.56 billion yuan, including the expenses of purchasing 25,279 new sets of technological equipment and of remodeling 289 product lines (Wu 1988, 10).

The "pollution fine" policy not only lends financial support to the environmental management to undertake more diversified functions for environmental control, but also helps old and new enterprises undertake technical reform to modernize their production lines and install high-technology–intensive equipment. Because of the technical reform and commodity adjustment, the water consumption, coal consumption, and industrial waste water drainage per ten thousand yuan output value were effectively kept under control (see figures 5.4 and 5.5 for illustration). A comparison of the numbers collected in 1985 with those collected in 1989, as indicated in figure 5.6, shows that the investment in the City Comprehensive Rectification Plan increased with the Gross Social Production Value. The

Figure 5.4
Water Consumption and Industrial Waste Water Drainage per Ten Thousand Yuan
Output Value, Guangzhou City, 1984–88

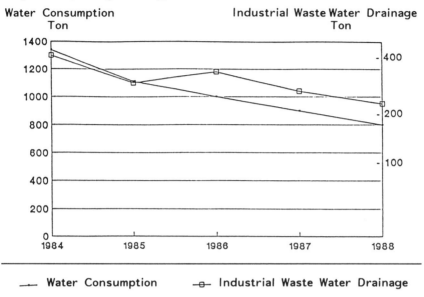

Water Consumption
Ton

Industrial Waste Water Drainage
Ton

___ Water Consumption   _◻_ Industrial Waste Water Drainage

Source: Guangzhou Environmental Monitoring Station.

Figure 5.5
Coal Consumption per Ten Thousand Yuan Output Value, Guangzhou City, 1984–88

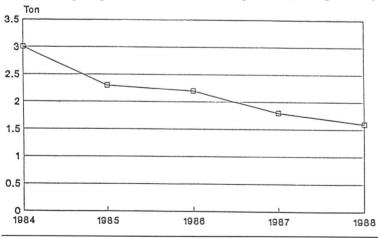

Ton

_◻_ Coal Consumption

Source: Guangzhou Environmental Monitoring Station.

Figure 5.6
**Gross Value of Social Output (GVSO) and Investment in the City Comprehensive
Rectification Plan (CCRP), Guangzhou City, 1985–89**

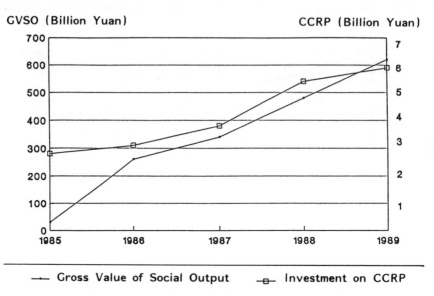

―•― Gross Value of Social Output   ―▫― Investment on CCRP

Source: Guangzhou Environmental Monitoring Station.

comparison indicates that with the rise of the Gross Value of Social Output, it
becomes financially viable for the Guangzhou environmental management to
consolidate and expand its environmental control capability.

It can be seen that the Guangzhou environmental management asserts the need
for economic development as the principal condition within which environmental
control must operate. In combining technical reform to deal with the sources and
nature of pollution, the management considers steadfast economic growth indis-
pensable to environmental control.

Making full use of the high economic growth rate in Guangzhou during the period
from 1983 to 1988, the Guangzhou environmental management was able to raise
more resources for rectifying the city's environment. Table 5.1 shows that the
total investment in the City Comprehensive Rectification Plan as a percentage of
the total domestic output value of Guangzhou increased and reached an all-time
high of 2.61 percent in 1988. Other prefectures and cities, however, maintained
a relatively low percentage level of around 1 percent to 1.5 percent in the same
period of time.

Figures 5.7 and 5.8 also establish the evidence that in the period from 1983
to 1988, when the total number of submitted investment plans increased, the amount
spent on fulfilling the requirement of the "three simultaneous points" policy also
increased substantially.

Table 5.1
Investment in the City Comprehensive Rectification Plan as a Percentage of the Total Domestic Output Value of Guangzhou City, 1983-88

Year	Percentage
1983	1.14
1984	1.72
1985	1.53
1986	2.10
1987	2.45
1988	2.61

Source: Guangzhou Environmental Monitoring Station.

The findings suggest that there is a correlation between economic growth and environmental policy expenditure variables in Guangzhou. From the viewpoint of organizational theory, economic growth lends financial support to the Guangzhou environmental management. Since the adoption of the "pollution fine" policy, the Guangzhou environmental management has sustained persistent administrative growth. The offices have employed more personnel, undertaken new projects, expanded and taken up new functions, and installed new technological equipment.

By expanding the domain of control, the Guangzhou environmental management can further absorb more financial support. It is likely that the management will place sustaining economic growth as the highest priority in environmental control. In this light, it is hard to imagine how the Guangzhou environmental management can put forward a full-fledged environmental control program.

POLICY IMPLEMENTATION STUDY REVISITED

Unfortunately, in using prevailing models of decision making to account for China's policy implementation problems, no single model incorporates the essential sociopolitical features that provide an understanding of the root causes of the nation's difficulty in achieving effective policy implementation. We do not, however, suggest that these models are of no use. In many instances a model is a simplification of reality, not a surrogate for it.

The rationality model offers one method of explaining implementation failure in China. Accordingly, the Chinese political system was portrayed as a centralized, monolithic, and powerful apparatus that could extend the impact of central power and central decision (Barnett 1967, 14-15). Criticisms exist, such as time constraints and the difficulty in obtaining full information requirements or a clear and ordered set of priorities (March 1978, 587-608; Kindler and Weiss 1978, 707-735). Subscribers to the rational model fail to probe and explore the decisional constraints faced by the top leaders. The foregoing analysis shows that in the course

Figure 5.7
Total Investment of Submitted Projects, Guangzhou City, 1983–88

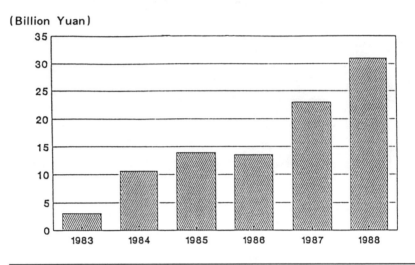

(Billion Yuan)

▧ Total Investment

Source: Guangzhou Environmental Monitoring Station.

of designing the national environmental control policy, the state must balance the need for maintaining high economic and social development and growth with the fundamental need for environmental protection. The two are equally important and competitive national objectives. As mentioned, in the zoning of the authority relationship and of financial management, the policy-making process is not as centralized, monolithic, and powerful as assumed.

Since power struggles and large-scale purges have been common throughout modern Chinese history, it has sometimes been suggested that policy outcomes are the results of power struggles. Furthermore, policy issues cannot be judged solely on intrinsic merits but also must be evaluated in terms of implications on individual leaders or factions (Elmore 1978, 199–203). Policy analysts must not underestimate the importance of the pursuit of and struggle over power as one of the core variables in Chinese politics.

The second approach—the power model—is not all-inclusive. A recent perusal of the policy arguments indicated that the diehard conservatives in the State Planning Commission urged that the reform measures be implemented in full throttle, despite the instability of the environment (Goh 1990, 13). Lucian Pye argued that the reforms over the last ten years have produced such large benefits that opposition to them would be considered eccentric. He further contended that the Chinese leaders disagreed among themselves on how to set the pace and direction

Figure 5.8
Total Investment in the "Three-Simultaneous Points" Policy, Guangzhou City, 1983–88

Thousand (Yuan)

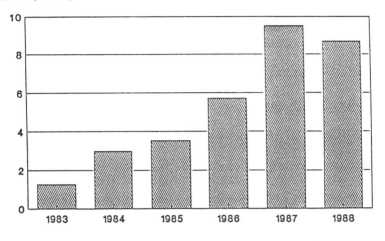

▨ Total Investment

Source: Guangzhou Environmental Monitoring Station.

of reforms, not on their *raison d'être* (Pye 1985, 182–215). It is worth noting that when resources are no longer centralized, power conflict may take a new shape and may take place outside the political mechanism. In fact, it has been well argued that policy does not necessarily emanate from the top decision-making body. Rather, it may be a response to stimuli, pressures, or problems (Mazmanian and Sabatier 1989; Davis and Mason 1982, 145–57; Palumbo and Harder 1981). On the field level, where the national administration (in this case, the National Ministry of Environmental Protection) seeks to unload the administrative as well as financial burdens, the local environmental management must contend with those people who have risen to power since the unfolding of economic reform in 1978. Pointedly, economic reform has created favorable conditions for environmental control in Guangzhou. It has raised revenues for expenses, for example, in updating technological processes and undertaking research and development in environmental science.

Unfortunately, economic reform has also created a "legitimacy crisis" for the environmental management in Guangzhou. The image accorded to a high-policy priority in sustaining economic development and growth confused the environmental bureaus. Our interviews indicated that members of the two offices responsible for environmental control in Guangzhou were at a loss in striking a balance between the needs of environmental control and those of economic development and growth.

From determining the nature and extent of pollution to be tolerated to quantifying the pollution discharge indices, there were, practically speaking, no standards. The importance of this problem may be gauged by considering the impact on both government-run and privately owned enterprises.

The continual reassurance of the need for economic development and growth creates a seemingly insurmountable barrier for the environmental management in promoting the need for and urgency of a "clean environment." It was not surprising to learn from our interviewees that environmental consciousness of the mass in Guangzhou is being described as "at bottom low." Those people rising up from economic reform and occupying important positions in society will fight against environmental management to protect their privileges, status, and whatever resources they have obtained under the disguise of promoting the nation's policy of sustaining economic development and growth.

A third approach attempts to complement the glaring deficiency of both the rationality and power models in treating the bureaucratic structure as some sort of black box and as a given. The Chinese bureaucracy is one of the oldest and largest bureaucracies in the world. Understanding Chinese politics may well enlighten one on how the structure affects the policy process, the elite struggle over power and policy. The bureaucratic approach argues that all policy outputs of organizations can be explained by the irreducible discretion exercised by officials and the operational routines that they develop to maintain their positions in organizations. Accordingly, decision making consists of controlling discretion and changing routine (Allison 1981; Halperin 1971). Oksenberg and Liberthal's seminal work on policy making in China presented findings more or less akin to the major propositions of the bureaucratic model (1988, 22–34). Applied to the environmental control in Guangzhou, the model leads us to see that environmental policies are largely results of agent-directed selection processes in highly complex multiorganizational situations. On reconsideration, we think that the bureaucratic model fails to search out some conditions that may alter the course of actions in implementing environmental control in China. Our research indicates that the units of analysis on environmental control in China must include people from the governmental agencies as well as individuals operating outside the boundaries of government. For example, the assessment of the policy, which demands polluters to absorb the social cost generated, requires an analysis balancing the likelihood that environmental management could guarantee the compliance of the polluters.

Concern about the policy's implementation problem stems from the recognition that policies cannot be understood in isolation from the means of their execution. Nonetheless, in most cases, it is impossible to say whether policies will necessarily succeed if given the appropriate means for attaining the assigned ends. Increasingly, policy analysts have begun to focus on the "process" by which policies are translated into administrative action. Due to the quality of our data and the narrowness of our investigation task, we prefer to simply explore the relevance of our findings and our understanding of China in order to develop a conceptual framework in examining the importance of "process" in the implementation problem of environmental policy in China.

In the formulation of environmental policy in Guangzhou, the ultimate necessity is recognized in the consideration of economic, technical, and sociopolitical feasibility. The process model proposed set out the parameters for policy analysts to discuss implementation problems in China. This approach grew out of the observation of some people, such as Douglas Bunker (1972), that the implementation process is being influenced at a finite number of key leverage points. We assume that the actual policy program is shaped in the implementation process, where individuals from governmental as well as nongovernmental units exchange their resources. The actors play around with and make use of the power factor, the resource factor, and the salience of an issue in reaching an agreement (Bunker 1972, 176).

To fully inform our readers, it is important to mention that the forty years of party domination in China have built up a society-wide informal authority structure paralleling and undercutting the authority of the formal one. Moreover, the informal authority structure has established a "political identity" shared among senior government and party cadres and extended toward every walk of life. When cadres with the "political identity" occupy leading positions in nongovernmental or privately owned enterprises, they create many social valves that impede policy implementation.

In environmental control in Guangzhou, the Guangzhou environmental management actively seeks hard to work with the nongovernmental and privately owned units. These are, however, also the "social units" that create great problems. The Guangzhou environmental management, for example, was not able to monitor "industrial waste water" discharged by the Guangzhou Paper Manufacturing Factory mainly because the administrative rank of the factory director was higher than that of the director in the Guangzhou Office of Environmental Protection. On another occasion, the environmental management could not undertake a site inspection of the Retired Air Force Personnel Recreation Club simply because many of the retired people in the club possessed a higher party seniority than that of the party general in Guangzhou. At the center of our observation is a distinctive social creature that we have called the "socially flattened organizational hierarchy," which enables those people with a political identity to bargain with the environmental management rather than to simply accept the authority.

Our study suggests that the distribution of power in a socially flattened organizational hierarchy, such as Guangzhou, is never stable. The key to understanding decisional and implementation constraints in Guangzhou's environmental control is to recognize that power is dispersed socially in such a way that no single unit of government is sufficiently powerful to force others, especially the nongovernmental units, to conform to a single concept of policy.

As long as genuine separation of party and state cannot be achieved, effective policy implementation cannot be attained. Although it is suggested that economic reform creates favorable conditions for environmental control, we argue that the present economic reform will further reduce the enforcement power of the Guangzhou environmental management in fighting against pollution. Since 1978, the economic reform has created a new social order in which the traditional values, such as job security, social status, and the concomitant privileges, are less attractive to bureaucrats and party cadres (Oi 1989, 201–33). In fact, they are losing their superior position vis-à-vis the nonelite groups in society. There has been a rise in "reform corruption." This represents an attempt by the bureaucrats and party cadres to divide the benefits of reform amid what John Kenneth Galbraith (1967) referred to as "public squalor, private prosperity" in an economic system with nascent market features. It is coupled with the resulting decentralization of decision making and the confusing message of according an equally high policy priority to economic development and growth and to environmental protection. Thus, we argue that the higher the level and the more rapid the pace of the economic development, the greater will be the difficulty that the Guangzhou environmental management will face in dealing with the pollution problem.

CONCLUSION

We began with the assertion that the policy implementation problem derives not only from the design of the policy but also from the relationship of the policy to the environmental setting. In studying Guangzhou's policy implementation problems, we explain the importance of the sociopolitical limits in determining outcomes, especially in the face of the economic reforms that seek to reduce the role of national administration and to delegate powers to local administration in China. The reform contributes to the further flattening of the social hierarchy, which, in turn, reduces the power of the environmental management in relating policy intent to outcome.

The analysis is a preliminary attempt to study the issue of implementation failure in China. We are not sure whether it is the idiosyncratic features that contribute to the implementation failure in Guangzhou. We are equally uncertain about the impact of economic reform on environmental protection in other places in China. We are not convinced that environmental control is bound to fail in China. There is no undoing of the past, but the failure offers an opportunity to come to terms with the complexities of environmental control in China.

Building on our preliminary observations, we suggest that future environmental policy study in China should be conducted by focusing on the nature of the socially flattened organizational hierarchy, the resources and power obtained by individuals outside the governmental units, and the mechanisms by which they adjust to each other's moves.

REFERENCES

Allison, Graham. 1981. *Essence of Decisions: Explaining the Cuban Missile Crisis*. Boston: Little Brown and Co.

Barnett, Doak A. 1967. *Cadres, Bureaucracy, and Political Power in Communist China.* New York: Columbia University Press.

Bunker, Douglas R. 1972. "Policy Sciences: Perspectives on Implementation Process." *Policy Studies* 3:171–80.

Chan, Hon S., K. C. Cheung, K. K. Wong, and Jack M. K. Lo 1990. "Environmental Consciousness, Policy Implementation, and Administrative Capacities in the PRC: Guangzhou, Zhengzhou, and Nanjing." Unpublished raw data.

Davis, Tom, and Charles Mason. 1982. "Gazing up the Bottom: Problems of Minimal Response in the Implementation of Manpower Policy." *European Journal of Political Research*, 145–57.

Elmore, Richard F. 1978. "Organizational Models of Social Program Implementation." *Public Policy* 2:185–228.

Galbraith, John Kenneth. 1967. *The New Industrial State.* Boston, Mass.: Houghton Mifflin.

Gan, Hai Zhang, Hon S. Chan, and Zheng Qi Wu. (1990). "A Study of the Application of Environmental Protection in China: Guangzhou as a Case Study." *Proceedings of the Conference on China and Hong Kong at a Crossroads: Prospects for the 21st Century.* Hong Kong Baptist College.

Goh, Keng Swee. 1990. "Governing China: The Experts Disagree." *Strait Times Weekly* (Overseas Edition), May 26.

Halperin, Morton. 1971. *Bureaucratic Politics and Foreign Policy.* Washington, D.C.: Brookings Institution.

Kindler, Donald R., and Janet A. Weiss. 1978. "In Lieu of Rationality: Psychological Perspectives on Foreign Policy Decision Making." *Journal of Conflict Resolution* 4:707–735.

Law of Environmental Protection. 1989.

——. Draft. 1979.

March, James A. 1978. "Bounded Rationality: Ambiguity and the Engineering of China." *Bell Journal of Economics* 2:587–608.

Mazmanian, Daniel A., and Paul A. Sabatier. 1989. *Implementation and Public Policy.* Lanham, N.Y. and London: University Press of America.

Oi, Jean. 1989. *State and Peasant in Contemporary China.* Berkeley: University of California Press.

Oksenberg, Michael, and Kenneth Liberthal. 1988. *Policy Making in China: Leaders, Structures, and Processes.* Princeton: Princeton University Press.

Palumbo, Dennis J., and Marvin A. Harder, eds. 1981. *Implementing Public Policy.* Lexington, Mass.: Lexington Books.

Pye, Lucian. 1985. *Asian Power and Politics.* Cambridge: Harvard University Press.

Qu Geping. 1990. "Using Law to Protect Environment and to Improve the Well-Being of People." *People's Daily*, May 9.

——. 1989. Report Speech. At the Third National Environmental Protection Conference, April 28, Beijing.

Qu Geping and Jin Chang Li. 1984. "Environmental Management." in Qu Geping and Woyen Lee, eds., *Managing the Environment in China.* Tycooly International Pub.

Wong, K. K. Kenneth. 1990. "The Environmental Protection Law in China: A Critical Review." Working Paper Series, Hong Kong Baptist College. (Original in Chinese.)

Wu Guang-lai. 1988. *Gai Gekai Fang Zhong De Guangzhou Huan Jing Bao Hu (The Environmental Protection in the Period of Economic Reform).* Guangzhou: Environmental Protection Dissemination Center.

CHAPTER 6

Economic Development and Decentralized Government

Thomas R. Dye

Thomas R. Dye describes the 1987 Report to the Thirteenth National Congress reaffirming the development of a strong socialist economy. One important reform was the separation of party functions from government functions and the separation of government functions from enterprise functions. He points to the trend of centralization and decentralization, arguing that state and local authorities are generally more effective in bearing the burden of most domestic programs. He provides useful structures and tables of the local government format of the PRC.

A problem in providing public goods and services is value determination. According to Dye, without an alternative forum for competitive prices, it is hard to assess the true value of goods and services. One key difficulty, despite the best of intentions, is that policymakers lack the necessary information to implement the maximum social-gain rule for determining the optimum level. Because they do not truly know the preferences of society, they cannot weigh or find the appropriate balance of benefits and costs.

Dye implicitly suggests that a major task of the government is to establish more responsive mechanisms for measurement and choice. This is indeed a call for implementable public policy. The new approach of requirements for provincial and municipal governments to raise their own funding provides a direct stake for the government in the success of the enterprise. It should now become possible for competition between the various provinces and municipalities to attract capital and labor. New businesses would now have the choice of locating in whichever area provided the best services at the lowest taxes. This competition is instructive because it helps to provide a measure of the preferences of enterprises and citizens for government activities. Support for such decentralized formats makes it possible to tailor policies to local conditions, thus providing much greater flexibility than offered by the more traditional centralized system. Dye concludes that decentralization permits rational policy evaluation. Pilot projects can be contrasted and compared.

One of the lessons that will be learned from this policy diversity is the useful comparison of alternative approaches to economic progress. Comparison across different nations is hindered by social and cultural differences. The relative homogeneity of China's provinces can make it easier to determine what works in examining economic performance, thereby generating conclusions of value to many government structures.

THE FUNCTIONS OF LOCAL GOVERNMENT

The issue of centralization versus decentralization has arisen often in the Chinese experience. Indeed, this experience has given rise to the following familiar observation: "Centralization leads to rigidity, while decentralization results in chaos; when the economy becomes chaotic it reverts to centralization, and when it becomes rigid, it reverts to decentralization" (quoted by He Jianzhang 1979, Xue Muqiao 1979, and others).

It is my argument that economic development is well served by decentralized government and that economic reform ought to include greater autonomy and independence for provincial, municipal, and regional governments (see figure 6.1). The Thirteenth National Congress of the Communist Party of China endorsed important economic reforms, including the separation of party from government functions and the separation of government from enterprise functions (Report 1987). These are vital reforms for advancing the economy of China. The decentralization of government authority without first separating governmental and enterprise functions would accomplish very little. If enterprises are not permitted to manage their own affairs, it would make little difference whether government controls were imposed by the central government or by provinces and municipalities. But it is also important that reform include decentralized governmental administration, less centralized bureaucracy, and greater flexibility for provincial and municipal governments to serve their local enterprises (see Communiqué 1984).

My observations derive from the study of the American federal system (Dye 1990). Despite many troublesome interventions by the government in Washington, the American states and their local subdivisions have proven to be much more efficient providers of domestic public goods and services than the national government. These governments provide almost all of the nation's public education, from elementary and secondary schools to colleges and universities. These governments are principally responsible for the nation's police and fire protection; sewage and solid waste disposal; public health and sanitation; transportation facilities, streets, and highways. They also provide most the nation's parks and recreational and cultural facilities and most of its prison and hospital facilities.

There are 82,341 local governments functioning in the United States: 50 states, 3,041 counties, 19,076 municipalities, 16,734 townships, 14,851 school districts, and 28,588 special districts. Collectively they spend about 10.4 percent of the gross national product, while the national government spends about 24.5 percent. In aggregate terms the role of the national government appears to overshadow that of state and local governments. But if expenditures for defense, interest on the national debt, and social security are subtracted from the national government's budget, what remains for all domestic programs in the national budget is only about 8.4 percent of the gross national product. Thus, state and local governments in the United States carry the major burden of domestic governmental programs.

How can the appropriate functions of provincial and municipal governments be determined? We must recognize that some important goods and services cannot be provided by independent enterprises under a pricing system. Both capitalist and socialist economies encounter practical difficulties in applying the law of value to some goods. These are "public goods," defined as services, activities, or functions that are nonexclusive in character—once they are provided to anyone, no one can be excluded from their benefits. These goods cannot be provided on the market because "free riders" who do not pay for them could enjoy them as much as those who do pay, via taxes or user fees. For instance, provincial and municipal governments must provide police and fire protection, road and street repair, sanitation and garbage disposal, and similar services.

Education is another public or nonmarket, because the whole society benefits from educating the young, not just the young themselves or their parents. The benefits of an educated population spill over to all citizens in the form of improved productivity, less social dependency, and greater prosperity for all. Similarly, many cultural, recreational, and social welfare activities benefit the entire community, not just those who participate directly. Welfare services, for people who are too old, sick, or disabled to contribute effectively to a market-based economy, are also public goods. We all might be willing to make private charitable contributions to assist these people, but if we do so individually and voluntarily, there is the temptation for others to get a free ride on our contributions. The free riders will benefit from seeing the old, sick, and disabled assisted without themselves contributing to the cost of the assistance. Finally, provincial and municipal governments might provide goods and services that constitute "natural monopolies," such as water and electrical supply and sewage disposal, where a large capital investment serves an entire community and where small competing enterprises cannot operate efficiently.

These theoretical guidelines—public goods and natural monopolies—are useful in determining the appropriate functions of government. However, there is a natural tendency for public officials to provide more public goods and services than required for efficient "service to the enterprises." It is natural for public officials to expand their budgets and personnel, to acquire more prestige and authority, and to provide more direction and regulation than required. This is true of *all* government officials, whether in socialist or capitalist systems. And it is true of officials in provincial and municipal governments as well as in central governments. The problem, then, is to construct a system of incentives to counterbalance the natural expansionist tendencies of public officials.

ENCOURAGING RESPONSIBLE LOCAL GOVERNMENT

Centralized government constitutes a monopoly over the provision of public goods and services throughout an entire nation; and a monopoly government has no direct way of determining the efficiency of its activities. In contrast, decentralized provincial and municipal governments, with independent responsibility for determining appropriate types and quantities of public services, allow us to compare performances among governments. Multiple governments offering different packages of services and costs to both citizens and enterprises within their jurisdictions provide comparative information to everyone about what public services can be offered at what costs.

If a provincial or municipal government performs well—that is, if it provides enterprises within its jurisdiction with quality public services at low costs—its enterprises should be able to develop more rapidly and show larger profits than enterprises in jurisdictions whose governments perform poorly. Admittedly, government policies are only one of the many potential influences on the growth of jobs, industry, and investments. Nevertheless, some information is better than none. A centralized, monopoly government receives little comparative information about the appropriate types and levels of public goods.

Responsible provincial and municipal government requires that all costs of public services provided by these governments be derived from revenues that the governments collect. If revenues are divorced from expenditures, then the services of these governments are separated from their costs. This separation is an invitation to irresponsible government.

If the central government provides all, or any significant portion, of the revenue of provincial and municipal governments, then the relation between the benefits and costs of public services provided by these governments is distorted. Provincial and municipal governments will be prompted to provide *more* public services than required for efficient operation of their jurisdictions, and they will continually press the central government for even higher levels of subsidies. In the United States, the national government currently provides about 18 percent of the revenue of state and local governments through a complex system of grants in aid. There is ample evidence that these revenues cause American local governments to oversupply public goods and services. Central government subsidies provide the wrong information to local governments, thus obscuring the true costs of public services.

By requiring provincial and municipal governments to raise their own revenues, these governments are given a direct stake in the success of the enterprises in their jurisdictions. If local government revenues are derived exclusively from taxes on the profits of local enterprises, then these governments will have a direct interest in the profitability of local enterprises. Increases in local government budgets, employment, and services, as well as growth in the status and prestige of local government officials, will depend on the success of their local enterprises. Thus, provincial and municipal officials will be given a direct incentive to assist enterprises within their jurisdictions in achieving high rates of growth.

The central government itself, by delegating more authority to local governments, will reduce its own share of tax revenues from enterprises. Provincial and municipal governments with authority to tax enterprises at whatever levels they choose will directly confront for themselves the tasks achieving efficiency, creating incentives, and encouraging initiative and hard work. If they set tax rates too high, or adopt progressive taxes penalizing the most profitable enterprises, then they risk impeding economic development in their jurisdictions. If they set tax rates too low, they cannot provide the essential infrastructure of transportation, energy, water, law enforcement, and social services required for a productive enterprise. It is true, of course, that local governments will make mistakes in judgment—usually in the direction of oversupplying public goods and overregulating enterprises. But comparisons of economic performance among provinces and municipalities allow both central and local government officials to observe the results of different economic policies. Mistakes can be more easily observed among multiple competitive governments than under centralized monopoly government.

MOBILITY AND ECONOMIC DEVELOPMENT

Mobility of capital and labor contributes to economic growth and efficiency. Permitting and encouraging enterprises and individuals to move about the country in search of the highest return on capital and labor improves the overall efficiency of the national economy. Moreover, the mobility of capital and labor provides additional incentive for provincial and municipal officials to offer the best packages of public services at the lowest costs. Decentralized government, combined with mobility of capital and labor, can create a "quasi-market" for public goods and services. Mobile enterprises and individuals can choose to locate in those provinces and municipalities that promise the best services at the lowest costs. It is true that many other factors besides the performance of local government will affect locational decisions, including transportation facilities, energy availability, labor force characteristics, and access to raw materials. But provincial and municipal government performance would be an additional consideration in locational decisions of freely choosing enterprises and individuals.

Competition among provinces and municipalities to attract mobile capital and labor would compel these governments to improve services and reduce costs. It would force these governments to make better estimates of the requirements of enterprises, both to attract new enterprise to their jurisdictions and to keep existing enterprises from moving away. New enterprises would have the option of locating in the province or municipality that promises the best package of public services at the lowest tax level possible.

Competition among provinces and municipalities would allow central government officials, enterprise managers, and individual citizens to compare governmental performances—to observe what services are offered at what costs in various provinces and municipalities. This comparative information is valuable in itself, but mobility of enterprises would give the system its driving force. Enterprises would have the opportunity to register their policy preferences by moving into or out of government jurisdictions or by simply staying put. Central government officials can watch the growth of various provinces and municipalities over time. Local government officials can evaluate their own performance against the performance of other local governments. A loss of capital over time, a decline in productivity and income, a loss of jobs, and a decline in the revenues of government would signal decision makers that they should search for alternative government policies.

COMPARING ECONOMIC DEVELOPMENT BY PROVINCE AND MUNICIPALITY

Evaluating the performance of any government requires accurate and reliable data. Enterprise managers and individual citizens, as well as central government officials, must enjoy ready access to census data, national income accounts, and government tax and expenditure data. Moreover, if the performances of autonomous provinces and municipalities and their governing officials are to be evaluated, accurate and reliable data must be provided for each province, municipality, and region over time.

In recent years, the People's Republic of China has made great progress in developing and publishing economic statistics (see, for example, *Almanac of China's Economy, 1985*). But data by province, municipality, and region is not always provided. Ideally, comparable data on all provinces, including Taiwan, Hong Kong, and Macao, would provide the best opportunity to evaluate economic performances.

An important argument for decentralized government is that it permits local policies to conform to local conditions. In a centralized system, one national policy is established for all, leaving little flexibility to adapt to local differences. The greater the variation in local conditions across a nation, the more appropriate becomes decentralization of government.

China's provinces, municipalities, and regions exhibit a great deal of variation in levels of economic development. According to the data provided in the *Almanac of China's Economy, 1985* for the year 1984, variation in per capita total social output ranged from a high of $2,243 in Shanghai to lows of $209 in Xizang, $207 in Guanxi, and $205 in Yunnan (see table 6.1). The coefficient of variation (a standardized measure of variation: that standard deviation divided by the mean) for per capita total social output among mainland provinces, municipalities, and regions is .91. (It is interesting to compare this coefficient to the coefficient of variation for per capita personal income among the fifty American states, which

Table 6.1

Per Capita Total Social Output and Industrial Output by Province, Municipality, and Region, 1984

	Total Social Output		Industrial Output	
	Per Capita (US$)	Change 83-84	Per Capita (US$)	Change 83-84
Beijing	1661	15.33	1158	10.46
Shanghai	2243	10.11	1932	9.70
Tianjin	1267	0.00	984	9.70
Anhui	281	43.98	113	15.18
Fujian	306	21.15	135	20.81
Gansu	276	10.54	152	11.22
Guangdong	393	19.00	196	26.53
Guizhou	N.A.	N.A.	78	17.90
Hebei	342	15.67	167	16.49
Heilongjiang	490	8.36	304	9.30
Henan	N.A.	N.A.	N.A.	N.A.
Hubei	413	19.02	230	14.88
Hunan	284	11.02	117	-10.87
Jiangsu	580	20.72	344	19.42
Jiangxi	N.A.	N.A.	N.A.	N.A.
Jilin	488	19.53	265	15.50
Liaoning	716	11.74	494	11.83
Zinghai	319	9.40	126	13.93
Shaanxi	N.A.	N.A.	N.A.	N.A.
Shandong	374	15.46	187	12.47
Shanxi	401	17.59	233	16.72
Sichuan	257	14.25	119	15.17
Yunnan	205	15.24	95	15.33
Zhejian	491	28.40	253	24.69
Guanxi	207	6.35	86	9.85
Neimongol	286	5.18	129	9.05
Ningxia	N.A.	N.A.	N.A.	N.A.
Xinjiang	339	11.22	139	11.91
Xizang	209	20.59	27	8.16
Taiwan	3010	8.90	1505	10.3
Hong Kong	5889	8.50	1778	16.1

Source: *Almanac of China's Economy, 1985*, compiled by the China Economic Compilation Committee and published by the Economic Management Publishing House in Beijing in December 1985. All the RMB figures have been converted to U.S. dollars at the rate of 3.2 yuan/1 dollar that prevailed from 1983 to 1984.

is only .14.) It Taiwan and Hong Kong are included in the computation, variation in levels of development is even greater; the coefficient of variation for all Chinese provinces is 1.45.

Variation in per capita industrial output among provinces and municipalities is even greater. Per capita industrial output ranged from a high of $1932 in Shanghai to a low of $27 in Xizang. The coefficient of variation for industrial output was 1.30. If Taiwan and Hong Kong are included in the analysis, the coefficient of variation is 1.27.

ECONOMIC DEVELOPMENT POLICY EVALUATION

A major advantage of decentralization in government is the opportunity it affords for policy evaluation. Multiple governments, with independent power to pursue alternative economic policies, provide surrogate "laboratories" for policy experimentation.

Measurement of change over time is critical to successful policy evaluation. Variations in *levels* of economic development among provinces and municipalities may be a product of many factors beyond the direct control of governments, factors such as the availability of raw materials, the cost of energy, access to markets, cultural limitations on the supply of skilled labor, or climate and environment. But variations in *rates of change* in output over specified time periods in any particular province or municipality may be more directly attributable to government policies. Observing rates of change in total social output and industrial output over specified time periods, in separate provinces and municipalities that pursue different development policies, facilitates evaluating the effectiveness of these policies.

To measure rates of change in output in each of China's provinces and municipalities, it will be necessary to develop accurate and reliable data on an annual basis for several years. The time span studied must be long enough to allow developmental policies to take effect and long enough to smooth out temporary fluctuations that might obscure underlying developmental trends.

Ideally, a systematic policy evaluation entails the close observation of output measures for adequate periods of time both before and after the introduction of specific economic reforms. And it entails the close comparison of provinces and municipalities that have pursued various economic reforms with those that have not, as well as the comparison of those that have pursued reform, with different degrees of comprehensiveness. It involves the careful measurement of both short-term effects and alterations in trend lines that forecast long-term change.

It is true that many factors besides government policies influence economic growth. Natural resources, history and culture, physical and human capital, geography, and even the weather can play a major role in determining economic growth rates among provinces. But with sufficient observations of economic output before the introduction of reform in any particular province or municipality, as well as sufficient postreform observations, it may be possible to control for many factors specific to each province or municipality. Sorting out the economic effects attributable to specific economic policies is never an easy task. But decentralization of government creates a natural laboratory.

Since the great Sichuan experiment in economic reform begun in 1978, the People's Republic of China has taken the lead in economic policy experimentation at the provincial level (Shambaugh 1982). The Sichuan experiment may have been centrally directed, and many adjustments may have been ordered by the central government (Lee 1986), but the principle of experimentation by province was vindicated.

Decentralization must mean more than just flexibility in the implementation of central government policies. Although it is undoubtedly true that decentralization makes government more manageable, provincial and municipal governments must be more than just administrative arms of the central government. Rather, they must have significant and autonomous responsibility for the economic progress of their jurisdictions. And it must be recognized that all provinces will not develop in the same fashion or at the same rate. A rigid commitment to ''equal development of all provinces'' would undermine local initiative and responsibility (see Pye 1981, chap. 5).

Policy diversity throughout all of China's provinces provides a unique opportunity for the world to observe and compare different approaches to economic progress. Comparative analyses across national economic systems are made very difficult because of the many cultural and historical differences among people. But comparative analyses of China's provinces can isolate differences in economic performance among people with common cultural and historical backgrounds (see Rabuska 1987). The effects of different government policies can be more easily identified against this common background. For this reason, government and peoples throughout the world are intensely interested in the results of China's experiments in economic reform.

REFERENCES

Almanac of China's Economy 1985. Beijing: Economic Management Publishing House, 1985.

Communiqué of the Third Plenary Session of the Twelfth Central Committee. 1984. ''Reform of the Economic Structure.'' (Reprinted in Harold C. Hinton, ed., *The People's Republic of China: A Documentary Survey*. Washington, D.C.: Scholarly Resources.)

Dye, Thomas R. 1990. *American Federalism: Competition among Governments*. Lexington, Mass.: Lexington Books.

He Jianzhang. 1979. ''Problems in the System of Planned Management of the Economy of Ownership by the Whole People in Our Country and the Direction of Reform.'' *Jingji Yanjiu*, no. 5, pp. 35–45. (Reprinted in *Chinese Economic Studies*, Summer 1980.)

Lee, Peter Nan-shong. 1986. ''Enterprise Autonomy in Post-Mao China.'' *China Quarterly* (March), 19–44.

Pye, Lucian. 1981. *The Dynamics of Chinese Politics*. Cambridge, Mass.: Oelgeschlager, Gunn, and Hain.

Rabuska, Alvin. 1987. *The New China: Comparative Economic Development in Mainland China, Taiwan, and Hong Kong*. Boulder, Colo.: Westview Press.

Report to the 13th National Congress of the Communist Party of China. 1987. Zhao Ziyang, ''Advance along the Road of Socialism with Chinese Characteristics.'' (Reprinted in *Beijing Review*, November 5, 1987.)

Shambaugh, David L., ed. 1982. ''Zhao Ziyang's 'Sichuan Experience': Blueprint for a Nation.'' *Chinese Law and Government* (Spring).

Xue Muqiao. 1987. "Socialism and Planned Commodity Economy." *Beijing Review*, August 17, 1987, pp. 14–19.
——— . 1979. "An Inquiry into the Problems Concerning Reform of the Economic System." Reprinted in *Chinese Economic Studies* (Winter 1983–84).

PART III

Policy Analysis Methods

CHAPTER 7

Super-Optimizing Analysis and Chinese Policy Problems

Stuart S. Nagel

Stuart S. Nagel presents a summary of key contemporary public policy problems in China subjected to super-optimizing analysis. The Super-Optimum Solutions (SOS) is a highly useful and creative approach to policy analysis problems whereby both sides come out ahead of their initial best expectations. The term *super-optimum* suggests that there are ways of, in fact, doing better than the best. Nagel describes transportation problems, food pricing, faculty compensation, and Hong Kong labor. His discussion centers on actual policy problems generated by policymakers and participants in government training institutes.

The technique of examining the positions from a liberal or conservative viewpoint provides a unique method of determining the characteristics that help define and clarify the SOS solution. It is analogous to the Mendeleyev table. Even when Mendeleyev did not know by direct experimentation what the next element would be, he knew what its characteristics would be. The issues that Nagel addresses, though specific in application, point to a larger resolution. The task for Chinese public administration and public policy is to enrich the capabilities of decision makers to solve any and all problems. The range of alternatives and the delineation of criteria make the analysis a comprehensive and thorough one. What is most important is that the technique can be summarized and transmitted in fairly short order with powerful results.

A question such as how can one improve the safety of bicycles at night illustrates such important factors of public policy evaluation as effectiveness, efficiency, equity, and feasibility. The SOS spreadsheet analysis is applied to food pricing, which, under the influence of Soviet economic theory, set low prices for agricultural products and high prices for industrial products. It is important to recognize that the emphasis here is not on the specifics of the issue but rather on the method that provides the keenest insight into political decision making. Nagel emphasizes the role of value and preferences in policy analysis, in addition to what can be easily measured or monetized.

An interesting example is how to increase faculty salaries without raising taxes. Nagel draws on solutions developed by Asian colleagues, including the ideas of establishing low tuition and increasing the number of students. The capability of a developing country is compromised if it cannot recruit and retain a superior faculty.

Nagel raises broader points of public policy evaluation by including concepts of third-party benefactors, impacts of gross national products, and the criticality of equity. The last issue that he addresses is Hong Kong's labor shortage. He draws together a number of alternatives and ends up by suggesting a broader definition of who should be employed, including the elderly, disabled, young mothers, people with part-time jobs, and those whose jobs and productivity could be increased. Nagel's guiding premise is the idea of solving problems by raising goals above the level generally considered the best. Above and beyond the specifics of the case examples he examines, the SOS approach provocatively suggests that one can, in fact, redirect one's thinking in terms of more innovative and responsive policy options.

The examples used in this chapter were largely generated as a result of the author's experiences in China and Hong Kong in 1989, speaking at such universities as Beijing University, the People's University of China, Sun Yat-Sen University, and Hong Kong University about systematic public policy analysis. The speaking tour also included groups of policymakers and governmental training institutes in Hong Kong, Guangzhou, and Beijing. At each place, the emphasis was on policy problems that the policymakers were actually dealing with rather than on hypothetical policy problems.[1]

BICYCLES VERSUS CARS IN BEIJING

The most exciting presentations in China were those that involved systematic policy analysis, decision-aiding software, multicriteria decision making, and super-optimum solutions. One example was the problem of how to deal with the sub-stantial and increasing quantity of nighttime accidents involving cars crashing into bicycles in Beijing and other Chinese cities. There are over seven million bicycles in Beijing, which means there are more bicycles in Beijing than there are people in any U.S. city except Los Angeles and New York.

The material that follows briefly describes how one might systematically analyze the basic alternatives available for dealing with the problem, the goals or criteria for choosing among the alternatives, and relations between alternatives and goals in order to choose or explain the best alternative, combination, allocation, or predictive decision-rule. The material shown in Table 7.6 includes both a verbal analysis and a computer output. The computer output involves a matrix, or table of columns and rows, in which the goals are in the columns, the alternatives are in the rows, the relations between goals and alternatives are in the cells, and the overall score for each alternative is at the far right. This system allows an analysis whereby one can determine what would be required to bring a second-place alternative or other-place alternative up to first place.

The Inputs

The Basic Alternatives (Table 7.1 and Figure 7.1)

1. Having reflectors on bicycles in order to decrease the number of nighttime accidents between cars and bicycles
2. Having battery-operated lights on bicycles; the word *having* in alternatives 1 and 2 means requiring by law
3. Doing nothing, just leaving things the way they are
4. Prohibiting bicycles at night
5. Giving away the reflectors free, at government expense, instead of having people buy the reflectors
6. Having people buy the reflectors, thus, alternative 5 and 6 are subdivisions of alternative 1, which requires reflectors but doesn't clarify who is going to pay for them
7. Requiring manufacturers and sellers of bicycles to install reflectors before the bicycles are sold
8. Subsidizing manufacturers to encourage them to put reflectors on bicycles
9. Requiring manufacturers to use reflective paint on bicycles so that the bicycles can be better seen at night by car drivers; using reflective paint costs no more than using regular paint; there is no extra cost involved, but there are a lot of extra benefits

The Criteria (Table 7.2 and Figure 7.2)

1. Reduce the number of accidents, especially where there are fatalities or personal injuries or even just property damage
2. Keep the cost down to the taxpayer and to society
9. Avoid solutions that unduly burden the poor, or stated more positively, seek solutions that do not discriminate against any major groups of people in terms of who benefits and who pays the costs (the third most important criterion, although ninth on the list)
3. Reduce the cost to the injured person and to the economy as a result of that person's productivity being lost
4. Reduce the cost with regard to the disruption of traffic, which could cause tieups in which everybody is late for wherever he or she is going
5. Reduce the cost to the government to send out an ambulance or a police car to take a police report; criteria 3, 4, and 5 are benefit items in the sense that if injuries are reduced, then there is no lost productivity, medical cost, disruption of traffic, or government involvement
6. Reduce the cost of equipment, such as what it would cost people to buy reflectors versus lights with batteries

Table 7.1
The Alternatives in the Beijing Bicycle Problem

Alternative	Alternative
1*FANGUANGJ.	1*REFLECTORS
2*CHE DENG	2*LIGHTS
3*BAOCHIYUANZHUANG	3*DO NOTHING
4*YEWANYANJINWAICHU	4*NO NIGHT BIKES
5*MIAN FEI FAN GUANG	5*FREE REFLECTORS
6*BI MAI FAN GUANG J	6*BUY REFLECTORS
7*CHANGJIA, SHANGREN BI MAIOU	7*REQUIRE MANUFACTURING
8*DUI CHANGJIA, SHANG REN DE BU TIE	8*SUBSIDIZE MANUFACTURING
9*XIN XING ZI XING C CHE ZUIJIAXUANZ	9*SOS

* These alternatives are being actively considered.

Figure 7.1
Grouping the Alternatives in the Beijing Bicycle Problem

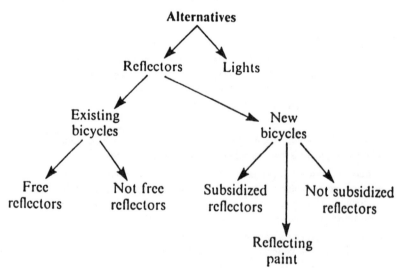

Table 7.2
The Criteria in the Beijing Bicycle Problem

Criterion	Meas.Unit	Weight	Criterion
1* JIAN SHAO SHI GU	1-5 FEN	1.00	1*+SAFETY
2* JIANG DI CHENG BEN	1-5 FEN	1.00	2*-COST
3 -SHANG HAI	1-5	1.00	3 -INJURIES
4 -JIAO TONG ZU SAI	1-5	1.00	4 -TRAFFICDISRUPTION
5 -JIU HU ZHI CHU	1-5	1.00	5 -AMBULANCE
6 SHE BEIG CHENG BEN	1-5	1.00	6 -EQUIP.COST
7 SHENG CHAN LI CHEN	1-5	1.00	7 -ENFORCE.COST
8 QIANG ZHI CHENG BE	1-5	1.00	8 -INTERFER.COST
9* GONG PING	1-5	1.00	9*EQUITY
10 ZHENG CE KE XING X	1-5	1.00	10 POLIT.FEASIBLE
11 GUAN LI KE XING X.	1-5	1.00	11 ADMIN.FEASIBLE

* These criteria are being actively considered.
+ These criteria are desirable to be increased.
− These criteria are desirable to be decreased.

Figure 7.2
Grouping the Criteria in the Beijing Bicycle Problem

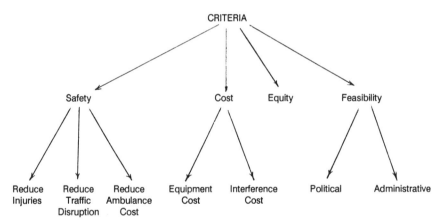

7. Reduce the cost of enforcement, since some solutions require more police enforcement than others

8. Reduce the cost of interference with the economy and productivity as a result of such solutions as prohibiting bicycles at night

9. Maintain equity (see above)

10. Maintain political feasibility, since different proposals have different degrees of likelihood of being adopted and some have no likelihood at all

11. Maintain administrative feasibility, since some proposals, like prohibiting bicycles at night, may be almost administratively impossible even if the proposal is adopted

Table 7.3

Relating the Nine Alternatives to the Three Main Goals

ALTERNATIVE/CRITERIA SCORING

	JIAN SHA	JIANG DI	GONG PIN	
1 FANGUANGJ.	4.00	3.00	0.00	1 REFLECTORS
2 CHE DENG	5.00	1.00	0.00	2 LIGHTS
3 BAOCHIYUANZHUAN	2.00	4.00	0.00	3 DO NOTHING
4 YEWANYANJINWAIC	5.10	1.00	0.00	4 NO NIGHT BIKES
5 MIAN FEI FAN GU	4.10	2.50	4.00	5 FREE REFLECTORS
6 BI MAI FAN GUAN	3.90	3.50	2.00	6 BUY REFLECTORS
7 CHANGJIA, SHANGR	4.30	3.70	0.00	7 REQUIRE MFG.
8 DUI CHANGJIA, SH	4.50	2.30	0.00	8 SUBSIDIZE MFG.
9 XIN XING ZI XIN	5.10	4.50	4.50	9 SOS

The Data Matrix

Looking at the greater detail from the data matrix in tables 7.3 and 7.6, go down the safety column from the highest total score to the lowest: (1) reflective paint; (2) battery-operated light; (3) subsidized reflectors put on by the manufacturer; (4) requiring manufacturers and sellers to put on reflectors; (5) free reflectors for existing bicycles; (6) requiring people to buy reflectors; (7) keeping things as they are.

Since there are nine alternatives altogether, two must have been left out. One is reflectors, which are worse in reducing injuries than lights but are less expensive than lights. Also left out was prohibiting bicycles at night, which would be near the top with regard to reducing injuries if it could be adopted and enforced.

The Outputs

The Overall Winner

The overall winner is to give free reflectors for existing bicycles but require manufacturers and sellers to put reflectors on future bicycles at their own expense, without a subsidy (see tables 7.4 and 7.6). That is the combination solution before considering the SOS, which outscores every alternative on every criterion, at least for long-run adoption: the reflective paint. This is a long-run solution, but there would be many existing bicycles that would need to be taken care of in the meantime. Therefore, the best solution would be free reflectors for existing bicycles and requiring reflective paint rather than reflectors for future bicycles, since reflectors are more expensive and less effective.

Analyzing the Alternatives in Groups

One could go down the cost to the taxpayer and society column in the same way. The best way to deal with this problem, however, is to go down the complete list of nine alternatives but to analyze them in groups.

First, compare reflectors and lights. Lights are better for reducing injuries; reflectors are cheaper. The important thing is that the analysis enables one to see what

Table 7.4
The Total Scores for the Nine Alternatives

Alternative	Combined Raw Scores	
1 FANGUANGJ.	7.00	1 REFLECTORS
2 CHE DENG	6.00	2 LIGHTS
3 BAOCHIYUANZHUANG	6.00	3 DO NOTHING
4 YEWANYANJINWAICHU	6.10	4 NO NIGHT BIKES
5 MIAN FEI FAN GUANGJ	10.60	5 FREE RELECTORS
6 BI MAI FAN GUANG J.	9.40	6 BUY REFLECTORS
7 CHANGJIA, SHANGREN	8.00	7 REQUIRE MFG.
8 DUI CHANGJIA, SHANG-	6.80	8 SUBSIDIZE MFG.
9 XIN XING ZI XING CH	14.10	9 SOS

the threshold figures are so that one can make a decision as to which alternative to adopt.

On the assumption that reflectors would win because they are less expensive and China is a poor country and the severity of the injuries is not so great in terms of the present number of fatalities, although they may be increasing, one rejects other more extreme alternatives, such as prohibiting bicycles or doing nothing. One also then analyzes how the reflectors should be paid for. One also then separately analyzes what to do about existing bicycles versus new bicycles. In that sense, items 1 and 2 are a pair, 3 and 4 are a pair, so are 5 and 6, and so are 7 and 8. We thus have a series of paired comparisons rather than having to face the more difficult question of which combination of nine alternatives is best. There may be a million, or at least many thousand, ways in which nine alternatives can be combined. However, we are interested only in the combinations, not the permutations. The answer would be to figure out how many different ways we could take nine things two at a time, nine things one at a time, nine things three at a time, and so on up to nine things nine at a time.

This is unnecessarily complicated, because so many of the combinations do not make sense. One needs to group various alternatives. If there are three pairs of supposed alternatives, then we eliminate three alternatives by deciding those three paired comparisons. This brings the total of nine down to six. It is more like a tree diagram than a series of paired comparisons. First, we decide between reflectors and lights. Then we subdivide reflectors into existing bicycles and new bicycles. Then we subdivide existing into free reflectors or not free. Then we subdivide new bicycles into those that have been subsidized to provide reflectors and those that are not subsidized. This requires us to make not a thousand different decisions among a thousand different combinations, but a grand total of three. We first decide reflectors rather than lights, and then we decide reflectors rather than free for existing bicycles, then we decide not subsidized rather than subsidized for new bicycles, and that is it.

The SOS does not apply to existing bicycles. It just adds a third alternative as to how to deal with new bicycles. We still have only three decisions to reach, except now the third decision has three alternatives instead of two.

Threshold Analysis and Multi-Dimensionality

The threshold analysis done on table 7.5 not only compares reflectors and lights, but does so in terms of exact figures showing how many lives will be saved and how many yuan will be required. The threshold figure is .40. Working with just the raw scores, reflectors win out over lights. If, however, instead of giving injuries and cost equal weight, one considers a half an injury to be worth 1,000 yuan, then there would be a tie. That is the same as saying that if one considers one injury to be worth 2,000 yuan, then there would be a tie. Thus, if a municipality considers one injury to be worth more than 2,000 yuan, then it should provide free lights instead of free reflectors. If it considers one injury to be worth less than 2,000 yuan, then it should go with the cheaper alternative of the reflectors. Thus, some cities that are wealthier than others could subsidize lights, and others could subsidize reflectors. Maybe no city would consider itself wealthy enough to subsidize lights. Maybe even no city would consider itself wealthy enough to subsidize reflectors. Or maybe all cities might be wealthy enough to subsidize lights, or at least reflectors.

This example illustrates several points: the importance of considering benefits, costs, and equity as the three main criteria of effectiveness, efficiency, and equity; the importance of also considering political and administrative feasibility; the usefulness of 1–5 scales if one has no better measurement available; the desirability of measuring in injuries saved and incremental monetary units if that kind of information is available; and the usefulness of developing a threshold expression for dealing with the kind of multidimensionality that occurs when the benefits are measured in injuries and the costs are measured in dollars or yuan. This example also illustrates the desirability of providing subsidies to increase compliance. At the same time, the incremental subsidy may be more expensive than the benefits from the incremental compliance. In other words, subsidies do increase compliance, but that does not mean that the subsidies are worth the cost in view of the fact that the increase may be trivial and the cost may be high. That is especially the case with regard to requiring manufacturers to comply with manufacturing standards in consumer products where safety is involved, as contrasted to requiring ordinary people to adopt something expensive on their own, like seatbelts or air bags. In other words, manufacturers can be required to comply with certain

Table 7.5
Comparing Reflectors and Lights on Lives Saved and Monetary Cost

THRESHOLD ANALYSIS

	CHEDENG	FANGUANGJI	Weight
JIANSHAOSHIGU	260.00	240.00	-0.400
JIANGDICHENGBEN	120.00	-40.00	-2.500

standards; they can be shut down if they fail to do so. It is harder to get compliance from individuals by ordering them to do something, as contrasted to simply giving them whatever it is they would otherwise be ordered to buy.

This example also shows the kind of SOS that dominates all the other alternatives on all the criteria. This SOS could be called a dominating SOS or simply a dominating solution. It lacks the key characteristic of a policy-oriented SOS because there is no strong liberal versus conservative split on reflectors versus lights. The liberal position would be that if reflectors are to be required, then they should be provided for free. A liberal position in this context might be to require automobiles to bear the burden of avoiding crashing into bicycles rather than putting the burden on the bicyclists to have either reflectors or lights. That, however, would be old-fashioned knee-jerk liberalism, which looks to what class of people should bear the burden rather than to what is required to get the job done. For example, car drivers could be required to get more powerful headlights at substantial expense, but that would probably be less effective incrementally in reducing accidents than requiring bicycle with cheap battery lights. The problem is that a bicycle with no reflectors and no lights is virtually impossible to see until it may be too late.

This problem also nicely illustrates how one can subdivide general criteria to be more specific if one wants to disaggregate into more itemized criteria and, likewise, with more specific itemized alternatives. Finally, the problem illustrates that one can have many alternatives and still not overwhelm the decision maker if the alternatives are grouped and sequenced so that at no time does the decision maker have to decide among more than three alternatives. The main thing about this example, however, is that it is a very real-world example suggested by real policymakers about a real problem with real data. (See table 7.6 for a review of all the criteria and alternatives.)

The Beijing bicycle problem thus illustrates such broader aspects of public policy evaluation as the role of effectiveness, efficiency, and equity as goals; the importance of considering political and administrative feasibility; the use of 1–5 scales for expressing relations between alternatives and goals; the need for dealing with multiple measurement on multiple goals; the usefulness of threshold analysis in dealing with both multidimensionality and missing information; using subsidies to increase compliance with the law; the nature of a dominating SOS solution that does better than the other alternatives on all the goals; working with groups of criteria; working with groups of alternatives; and the importance of working with realistic problems.

FOOD PRICES IN CHINA

An SOS Spreadsheet Perspective

High farm prices is the conservative alternative in this context, and low prices is the liberal alternative (see table 7.7). The liberal weights involve a 3 for urban

Table 7.6
The Problem of Collisions between Bicycles and Cars

CRITERIA / ALTERNATIVES	L Goal +Safety	C Goal -Cost	L Goal Equity	N Goal Political Feasibil.	N Goal Admin. Feasibil.	N Total Neutral weights	L Total Liberal weights	C Total Conserv. weights
L Alternative Reflectors	4	3				14	15	13
L Alternative Lights	5	1				12	16*	8
C Alternative Do Nothing	2	4				12	10	14*
C Alternative No Night Bikes	5.1	1		1	1	12.2	16.3	8.1
L Alternative Free Reflectors	4.1	2.5	4			21.2	25.8*	15.6
C Alternative Buy Reflectors	3.9	3.5	2			18.8	21.2	16.4*
L Alternative Require Manufacturer	4.3	3.7				16	16.6*	15.4*
C Alternative Subsidize Manufacturer	4.5	2.3				13.6	15.8	11.4
S Alternative SOS	5.1	4.5	5			19.2	19.8**	18.6**

NOTES:

1. C = conservative; L = liberal; N = neutral; and S = super-optimum solution.
   *Conservative or liberal winner without the SOS.
   **Conservative or liberal winner considering the SOS.

2. The benefits of increasing safety include reducing injuries, reducing traffic disruption, and reducing ambulance costs. The components of the cost variable include equipment costs and enforcement costs, and interference costs. Scores are not shown on those goals because they are subgoals of the main goals of safety and cost, although scores could be shown if one wants further details.

3. Scores on the equity goal are only shown and added for comparing free reflectors with buying reflectors since that is where the equity goal is mainly involved. Likewise, scores on the feasibility goals are only shown for prohibiting bicycles at night since that alternative is not politically or administratively feasible.

Table 7.7
Pricing Food in China and Elsewhere

CRITERIA	C Goal Rural Well Being	L Goal Urban Well Being	N Goal Admin. Feasibility	N Goal + Farming Methods	N Goal + Export	N Goal Import Technology	N Goal + GNP	N Goal Political Feasibility	N Total Neutral weights	L Total Liberal weights	C Total Conserv. weights
ALTERNATIVES											
C Alternative											
High Price	5	1	3	4	4	4	4	1	52 (18)	48 (14)	56* (22)
L Alternative											
Low Price	1	5	3	2	2	2	2	5	44 (18)	48* (22)	40 (14)
N Alternative											
Compromise	3	3	3	3	3	3	3	3	48 (18)	48 (18)	48 (18)
S Alternative											
Price Supplement	5.1	5.1	3	5	5	5	5	5	76.4 (26.4)	76.4** (26.4)	76.4** (26.4)

Notes:

1. The intermediate totals in parentheses are based on the first three goals. The bottom-line totals are based on all the goals, including the indirect effects of the alternatives.

2. The SOS of a price supplement involves farmers receiving 101 percent of the price they are asking, but urban workers and others paying only 79 percent, which is less than the 80 percent they are willing and able to pay.

3. The difference of 22 percent is made up by food stamps given to the urban workers in return for agreeing to be in programs that upgrade their skills and productivity. The food stamps are used to pay for staple products (like rice or wheat) along with cash. Farmers can then redeem the stamps for cash, provided that they also agree to be in programs that increase their productivity.

4. Food stamps have administrative feasibility for ease in determining that workers and farmers are doing what they are supposed to do in return for the food stamps. They cannot be easily counterfeited. They serve as a check on how much the farmers have sold.

5. By increasing the productivity of farmers and workers, the secondary effects occur of improving farming methods, increasing exports, increasing importing of new technologies, and increasing the GNP.

6. High prices are not politically feasible because of too much opposition from workers who consume but do not produce food. However, the high prices are acceptable if they can be met by way of price supplements in the form of food stamps.

C = conservative; L = neutral; and S = super-optimum solution.
* Conservative or liberal winner without the SOS
** Conservative or liberal winner considering the SOS

105

desires, a 1 for rural desires, and a 2 for all the other goals. With the liberal weights, the SOS wins 76 to 48 for all the other alternatives. We then go back and put in the conservative weights. The conservative weights give a 2 to all the neutral goals just as liberal weights do, but they do a flip-flop on urban and rural desires. For the conservative in the context, rural desires get a 3 rather than a 1, and urban desires get a 1 rather than a 3. The SOS is a winner even with the conservative weights, although now the high prices do better than they did before but still not as well as the SOS.

The neutral perspective is not to give everything a weight of 1 but rather a weight of 2. If the neutrals gave everything a weight of 1, they would be giving neutral goals less weight than either the liberals or the conservatives give them. Thus, in the neutral picture, rural desires get a weight of 2 and so do urban desires. To the neutral, everything gets a weight of 2. The SOS wins with the neutral weights too. It is super-optimum because it is out in front over both the conservative and liberal alternatives using both the conservative and liberal weights. It also wins over the compromise. The SOS involves the farmers getting better than high prices and the urbanites paying lower than low prices, with the government providing a supplement like the minimum-wage supplement, provided that administrative feasibility is satisfied.

Administrative feasibility involves the use of food stamps. They are given to urban food buyers. They cannot be easily counterfeited. Food buyers give them to retailers, who give them to wholesalers, who give them to farmers, who turn them in for reimbursement. Criterion 8 talks about political feasibility. There should be a separate criterion for administrative feasibility.

Of special importance is that no farmers get the supplement unless they agree to adopt more modern farming methods. Otherwise, the supplement is just a handout for subsidizing inefficient farming. With the adoption of more modern farming methods, productivity goes up. Food becomes available for export. Foreign exchange then gets acquired for importing new technology. The new technology increases the GNP, and everybody is better off, including the taxpayers who pay the supplement. They are better off because, with the increased GNP, the government can even reduce taxes if it wants to do so. It can reduce taxes below a 20 percent level and still have more tax revenue if the GNP base has substantial increases.

An Economic Perspective

The food price has long been a big problem in China.[2] Since the foundation of the People's Republic of China, the government, as influenced by the Soviet economic model, had adopted the policy of extremely low pricing of agricultural products and high pricing of industrial products. That meant a big gap between the price of industrial products and that of agricultural products. The farmers paid a high "tax rate" through the form of a low selling price. For this reason, the farmers got little profit from agricultural production, which in return meant that the farmers did not have enough financial input in farming. This led to the shortage of agricultural products.

At the low price of p_0 farmers were only willing to produce and sell agricultural products at the quantity of q_0. If the price was settled by market, the equilibrium quantity would be q_1, the price would be p_1, and Δ_q, which is the gap between q_1 and q_0 would be the shortage (see figure 7.3).

What the urban people want from agriculture is an abundance of farm food products at a reasonably low cost, whereas the farmers want to sell their products at a possibly high price. This is the conflict met by the government in the agricultural policy-making process, the solution to which can be used as an example of a super-optimum one.

We give the grains price as an example. The producers wish to sell at the price of fifty fen per kilogram ($\$1 = 3.78$ yuan $= 378$ fen), whereas the highest price acceptable to the consumers if thirty fen per kilogram, as figure 7.3 shows. The line C'C indicates that along with the decreasing of the grain price, it will cost the consumers less to buy the grains. That is to say, the consumers' benefit will increase. The line OF illustrates that the higher the price of the grains the farmers sell, the more benefit they will receive, and vice versa. If the price at which the farmers sell their products is fifty fen per kilogram, and the price at which consumers buy is thirty fen per kilogram, both of the two sides can get the benefit of B_0. The compromise price would be forty fen per kilogram, at which the consumers or the farmers might get the benefit of B_1. It might be a loss for both consumers and farmers. (As figure 7.3 indicates, B_1 and B_0.) It is a loss to farmers if the fifty fen per kilogram is the minimum price for them to cover the cost of the production. The forty fen per kilogram is a loss to consumers if the thirty fen per kilogram is the maximum price that they can afford to pay at their present wages.

A super-optimum solution to this problem might involve raising the price at which the farmers sell their products to sixty fen per kilogram but simultaneously requiring consumers to pay only twenty fen per kilogram. The forty-fen difference would be paid by the government through the food price subsidies. The government would collectively buy the agricultural products from farmers at the price of sixty fen per kilogram, then sell them to urban people at the price of twenty fen per kilogram. At this situation, as figure 7.3 shows, the benefit that the consumers or the farmers might get increases from B_1 to B_2, and B_2 is higher than B_0, which indicates that through the government subsidies, both the consumers and the farmers can get a higher benefit than their best expectation.

But what can the third-party benefactor, the government, get from this program? It seems that the subsidies would increase the government expenditure and deficit, but actually the government could come out ahead. This is so by virtue of the following.

1. The increase in the supply of agricultural products, shown in figure 7.3. If the new price p_2 is higher than the original price p_0 and the equilibrium price p_1, the supply

Figure 7.3
An Economics Perspective on the Food Pricing SOS

1A. SUPPLY AND DEMAND FOR FARM PRODUCTS

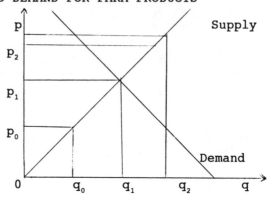

1B. PRICE AND BENEFITS

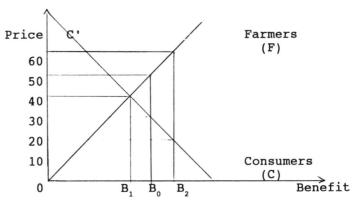

1C. INCREASED SUPPLY

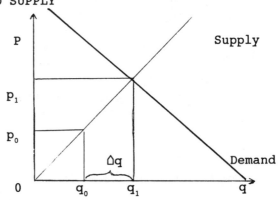

of the agricultural products will increase from q_0 to q_2. This not only will resolve the shortage problem but also may make the country become a food exporter.

2. The increase in input to the land by farmers. This in return will reduce the government investment on agriculture.

3. The decrease in the inflation rate. This is very important for the economic reform and development of China.

In fact, the beginning of the economic reform of China was in the rural areas in the later 1970s, with the adoption of the Family-Contract-Responsibility-System in agricultural production and the increase of the price of the agricultural products that the government bought from farmers. From 1980 to 1984, the quantity of the crops production reached the highest point in Chinese history. But since 1985, the agricultural economic growth has stagnated. The reasons might involve many aspects, but one of the important factors leading rural economy to this situation is the increase in the price of the industrial products that are used in farming, such as farm machinery, seeds, fuels, and pesticides. The benefit that farmers got from the rising of the price of agricultural products has been covered by the increase in the cost of the agribusiness input. To change this situation, the government has made the decision to increase input on agriculture. New agricultural policies are expected to be made and implemented in the 1990s.

A Reaction to the Food Pricing SOS

A social scientist from a prominent international organization came up to me after a presentation in Morocco. He said he could not accept the idea of a food supplement that would make both the rural farmers and the urban workers simultaneously better off in developing countries. He said that according to the example, the farmers in China wanted 20 cents per pound for rice and the workers wanted to pay only 10 cents per pound. A compromise would have been 15 cents per pound. The food supplement would have paid the farmers 21 cents per pound, and the workers would have had to pay only nine cents per pound. He objected on the grounds that he had recently been to China and the price of rice was not what I said it was.

The chair of the panel told him that the exact prices might be an irrelevant consideration. He should just view this as a hypothetical problem to see the big picture with regard to the idea that a third-party benefactor could make both sides come out better. The chair suggested that instead of twenty cents per pound for rice he could use algebraic symbols and that maybe he could see what was happening better.

That did not seem to help. The problem was that this international organization had spent large amounts of money trying to come up with solutions for exactly this kind of problem. His mind apparently was so narrowly focused that he refused to recognize any kind of solution that he had not thought of or that other people at his institution had not thought of. Therefore, he clutched for whatever straw he could find to argue that this was not a solution.

The moral of the story is not to provide any straws. One has to be careful about the details, even if the details are irrelevant. For instance, the correct figure is $200 per week (instead of $800 per month) for the subscription fulfillment and related costs of the Policy Studies Organization. Which figure one uses makes no difference at all in comparing a set of alternative proposals. Nevertheless, someone like this international executive will say we cannot accept this analysis because the correct figure is really $200 per week and not $800 per month. And the correct figure for a pound of rice in China as of July 20, 1989, when the presentation was made, was actually about twelve cents per pound. I said it was somewhere between ten and twenty cents, implying that it was fifteen cents. If an intelligent international executive could say that this destroys the whole idea of super-optimum solutions, then less intelligent, less knowledgeable people might be even more likely to find a defense mechanism. Such a mechanism enables them to avoid admitting, explicitly or implicitly, that they might have been scooped on a solution. It also avoids allowing the opposition to come out ahead regardless of how well one's own side comes out.

RAISING FACULTY SALARIES WITHOUT RAISING TAXES IN CHINA

This example was developed at People's University and Beijing University by Professor King Chow and Lu Junwei, a graduate student. The example involves the dispute between the government and university professors in China over faculty salaries (see table 7.8). The professors have been seeking a salary of approximately 300 yuan for a certain time period. The government has been willing to give, at the most, 200 yuan. The object is to come up with a way in which the faculty members could be paid more than 300 yuan but the government would be able to pay even less than 200 yuan.

The solution developed by Chow, Lu, and others is to institute a system of low tuition throughout the Chinese universities while simultaneously increasing the number of eligible students. The money obtained could be used to pay faculty salary increases without having to draw on the government's limited resources. Provision could be made for low-income students to receive scholarships or loans, especially loans that would be forgiven if the students go into fields of work that are in short supply. The result would be salaries higher than 300 yuan for faculty, with a possible reduction of the government's contribution to less than 200 yuan. More people would also receive college educations, to the benefit of national productivity, which in turn would bring in increased national income and more government revenue.

This is an example of a super-optimum solution in which everyone comes out ahead. The low faculty salaries have also been a point of antagonism between the government and graduate students who anticipate becoming professors,

Table 7.8
Evaluating Policies Concerning Chinese Faculty Salaries

CRITERIA / ALTERNATIVES	L Goal Attract Faculty	C Goal -Cost of Government	L Goal Equity to Students	N Goal +Educated Population	N Goal +GNP	N Goal Political Feasibility	N Total Neutral weights	L Total Liberal weights	C Total Conserv. weights
L Alternative Faculty Demand	4	2	3	4	4	2	38 (18)	43 (23)*	33 (13)
C Alternative Government Offer	2	4	3	2	2	4	34 (18)	35 (19)	33 (17)*
N Alternative Compromise	3	3	3	3	3	3	36 (18)	39 (21)	33 (15)
S Alternative Tuition and Scholarships	5	5	4	5	5	5	58 (28)	62** (32)	54** (24)

NOTES:

1. For those who prefer numbers to words, the faculty demand can be thought of as 300 monetary units, the government offer as only 200 units, and the compromise as 250 units.

2. The super-optimum solution consists of the government paying the faculty 190 monetary units, but the faculty receiving 310 monetary units. The difference comes from establishing a low-tuition system to replace the current non-existent tuition system. The low tuition system would provide for scholarships and other forms of student aid for those students who cannot afford the tuition. The SOS would also allow for larger student enrollment without lowering admission standards.

3. The intermediate totals in parentheses are based on the first three goals. The totals not in parentheses are based on all six goals including the indirect effects of the alternatives.

C = conservative; L = neutral; and S = super-optimum solution.

* Conservative or liberal winner without the SOS

** Conservative or liberal winner considering the SOS

especially when sellers of orange soda pop and cucumbers can make more in a few days than a university faculty member makes in a month.

The Chinese faculty salaries problem thus illustrates several broader aspects of public policy evaluation. First, having a third-party benefactor is a useful way of arriving at super-optimum solutions, but the third-party benefactor does not have to be the government. That is especially so when the government is one of the two main parties. In this context, the third-party benefactor was in effect the students, who pay tuition.

Second, it is important to consider the side effects of an SOS solution on the gross national product. Those side effects include the following: (1) the multiplier effect, which occurs as a result of increased income causing increased income for numerous other people via a chain of spending; (2) the compound interest effect, which occurs from an increase in the base to which next year's growth rates are applied, similar to getting compound interest on interest; (3) the intergenerational effect as a result of improving parental role models; (4) the taxpaying feedback effect due to the increased GNP generating more tax money and subsidy money even if the tax rate is constant or lowered; (5) the export surplus effect, which occurs via a productivity surplus that is available for export to obtain new capital goods and technologies that further increase productivity; and (6) the welfare reduction effect, whereby the prosperity of an increased GNP means less of a burden on the government to provide for unemployment compensation, public aid, public housing, food stamps, Medicaid, and other forms of welfare. These six points emphasize the upward-spiral benefits of investing in human resources and new technologies for increasing the gross national product.

Finally, it is important to consider equity, and not just effectiveness and efficiency, in evaluating alternative public policies. It is ironic that equity may be considered more in an affluent capitalistic society than in a hard-pressed Marxist society, even though Marxism in theory is supposed to be more sensitive to the spread of benefits and costs across economic classes and ethnic groups.

THE HONG KONG LABOR SHORTAGE

The Problem

When the author spoke before the Hong Kong government, the officials in effect said that they did not especially want to hear about solar energy versus nuclear energy, or trials versus pleas, or getting married, or any of those other examples. They wanted to know about a SOS to a problem involving Hong Kong, a crucial problem that they were not able to work out.

The labor shortage was such a problem, which government officials were approaching from a very traditional perspective. One alternative was to import additional labor. This actually required no importing at all. All it required was to stop arresting people seeking to cross the borders from every direction. These include the Vietnamese boat people, the people from the Chinese mainland, the

Filipinos, and even some people from English-speaking places (although not many) like Australia, Britain, or India. Most English-speaking people are a little cautious about settling or staying in Hong Kong given that it will become a Chinese province in 1997.

The shortage thus created a dilemma that paralyzes decision making if the choice is one of retaining the labor shortage and thereby missing out on opportunities to make Hong Kong even more prosperous than it is, versus allowing labor in and thereby diluting the population of Hong Kong. This is partly a racist problem but is also a legitimate concern, for a lot of expense is involved in education and welfare, although the immigrants may be especially ambitious people who in the long run will pay more than their share of taxes. This may be especially true of the Vietnamese boat people, although coming by boat from Vietnam to Hong Kong is not much more difficult than crossing the border from Mexico to Texas. They are, however, giving up whatever they had in Vietnam.

The SOS that seemed to be a kind of blind spot by virtue of how the terms were defined is simply to redefine the labor force. Redefining the labor force means recognizing all the potential labor: elderly people who are capable of working but are not doing so, disabled people, mothers of preschool children, people with part-time or seasonal jobs, people who are looking for second jobs, and especially people whose jobs and productivity could be upgraded.

The SOS Table for Conservatives and Liberals

The alternatives in table 7.9 are (C1) import cheap labor; (C2) preserve national purity; (L1) preserve union wages; (L2) provide immigrant opportunities; (N) import some labor but less than either C1 or L2 would like but more than C2 or L1 would like; or (SOS) add to the labor force and increase labor productivity. The SOS sounds a bit ambiguous, since one can add to the labor force by importing labor. In this context, it means adding by drawing on people who are already part of the society.

One key goal would be to increase the GNP, especially by filling orders that otherwise would not be filled. A second key goal is to minimize disruption to the existing society. It looks as if a general pattern tends to be emerging in developing these tables: having one relatively liberal goal and one relatively conservative goal, with other goals being relatively less important or unimportant.

The scoring tends to show the conservative alternative being mildly negative on the liberal goal and mildly positive on the conservative goal and the opposite with the liberal alternative. The neutral alternative goes in the middle on both goals, and the SOS alternative does especially well on both goals.

In this example, there are two conservative alternatives and two liberal alternatives. It is not appropriate to say that one conservative alternative is more conservative than another and that one liberal alternative is more liberal than another. They are just two different kinds of conservatism and two different kinds of liberalism. One kind of conservatism is basically probusiness and is interested

Table 7.9
The Asian Labor Shortage

CRITERIA ALTERNATIVES	C_1L_2 Goal + GNP	C_2L_1 Goal -Disruption to Society	N Total Neutral weights	Total L_1 & C_2 Weights (Nativism & Unionism)	Total L_2 & C_1 Weights (Open Door Policy)
C_1 Alternative Import Cheap Labor	4	2	12	10	14*
C_2 Alternative Preserve National Purity	2	4	12	14*	10
L_1 Alternative Preserve Union Wages	2	4	12	14*	10
L_2 Alternative Provide Immigrant Opportunities	4	2	12	10	14*
N Alternative Import Some Labor	3	3	12	12	12
S Alternative + Labor Force + Productivity	5	5	20	20**	20**

Notes:

1. Business conservatives welcome cheap labor to decrease expenses and increase profits. Cultural conservatives resist easy immigration as being disruptive to national purity.
2. Union liberals resist immigration as being disruptive to union wages. Intellectual liberals like to provide ambitious immigrants with opportunities to succeed.
3. By relieving the labor shortage, immigration increases the gross national product. There is, however, some disruption in absorbing the new immigrants.
4. The SOS alternative involves increasing the labor force by upgrading the skills of the elderly, the disabled, and mothers of preschool children; by making better use of people who work part-time or seasonally, or who could use a second or better job; and by increasing the productivity of present workers through new technologies and training.

C = conservative; L = neutral; and S = super-optimum solution.
* Conservative or liberal winner without the SOS
** Conservative or liberal winner considering the SOS

in maximizing business profits. The other kind of conservatism is basically nationalist bordering on racist and is more concerned with ethnic purity than with profits. One for a 2 on the second goal, or a 3 on both.

The liberal totals in this context favor alternatives C1 and L2. That depends on what kind of liberal we are talking about, though. Maybe we have to say that both goals are ambivalent goals. An increased GNP is normally a liberal goal but would be opposed by unionists in this context if it means importing cheap competitive labor. Therefore it would be a liberal goal only in the eyes of the L2 liberals. It is also a conservative goal in they eyes of the C1 conservatives. This could be a good example of where it is not meaningful to refer to the goals as being conservative or liberal.

Each goal is supported by both liberals and conservatives intensely, but different kinds of liberals and conservatives. In the usual situation, all goals are supported by liberals and by conservatives, but the liberals like some goals relatively better than the conservatives do and vice versa. Here it is not that the liberals like some goals relatively better than the conservatives do. It is that some liberals like some of the goals better than other liberals do. Likewise, some conservatives like some of the goals better than other conservatives do. In other words, there is a kind of conflict within conservatives on the goals as well as on the alternatives, and it might thus be meaningless to talk about a liberal total and a conservative total. One could talk about an L1 liberal total and an L2 liberal total and a C1 conservative total and a C2 conservative total. In that regard, increasing the GNP is a C1 goal and an L2 goal. Decreasing societal disruption is a C2 and an L1 goal.

That complicates the assigning of weights a bit, but not that much. Table 7.9 shows how each group would weight the goals. Knowing that, we can calculate in our heads what the totals should look like. The subtotals could be put on the table. There are only two multipliers, namely 3 and 1. It is easy enough to show what each relation score becomes when multiplied by 3 and when multiplied by 1. We do not have to write anything down to show what each raw score becomes when multiplied by 1.

Calculating the four sets of new totals, for the L1 or unionist set, the winner is either preserve national purity or preserve union wages. They both amount to the same thing in terms of whether external labor should be excluded or imported. One could say that racist conservatives and exclusionary unionists are strange bedfellows. But there is nothing very strange about that at all. It has occurred many times in American history where otherwise economic-liberal union members would take sexist or racist positions.

The L2 or civil libertarian column has intellectuals and businesspeople joining together because they share a willingness to allow for more open immigration, even though their reasons may be different.

On the C1 or business column, the results turn out to be the same as the L2 column because in the context of this subject matter and these goals, the businesspeople who want to import cheap labor come out with the same totals as the intellectuals who want to provide more immigrant opportunities. We can get differences in those columns if we add a goal like "increase individual firm profits," which would please the business types but not necessarily the intellectual types. If we add a goal called "reward ambitious immigrants," that would please the intellectual types but not necessarily the business types. We would have to add two goals like that in order to get a difference between the L2 column and the C1 column. We would then have to add 2 more goals to get a difference between the L1 and the C2 column.

The C2 or nativist column, which reflects the goals of those who want to preserve national purity, comes out the same as the L1 column, which reflects the goals of those who want to preserve union wages. We could force C2 and L1 to be separate in the United States by adding a goal like "encourage white Anglo-Saxon Protestantism." That might please those who want to preserve national purity, but it would not please the average unionist who tends to be Polish, Italian, Irish, Hispanic, or otherwise Catholic. Likewise, we could add a goal that would please the unionists but not please the ethnic purity people. All we have to do is add a goal that is the opposite of encouraging white Anglo-Saxon Protestantism, such as encouraging diversity of religion and language in the United States. That is the opposite of preserving national purity, but it would be likely to please most unionists since they tend to be minority group people, at least in terms of religion if not race.

All this can be said verbally without cluttering up the table by adding four more goals. As of now, the table has seven columns. That would give it eleven columns, which is not so horrendous, although the standard table allows for only nine. A main reason for not adding those goals is not because they would make the table too complicated but because they are not as relevant to the immigration issue as the goals that we currently have. We could add just two more columns, since there is no reason why we have to add one column that talks in terms of promoting a single ethnic group (versus pluralism) and then another column that talks in terms of doing the opposite.

The best way to handle the problem is to just note that although the L1 and C2 groups come out with the same bottom line, as do the L2 and C1 groups, they do so for different reasons. This table is not designed to explicitly indicate what those different reasons are. It is designed to bring out which alternative is the best in light of the alternatives available and the goals to be achieved. The verbalization can discuss the motives behind why different groups may place the same high value or low value on a goal for different reasons. It can also say why two groups have the same reasons but yet are different groups because they differ with regard to other matters.

The SOS Alternative

Instead of concentrating on the diversity within conservatives and liberals, we could put more emphasis on the idea of solving the problem by raising goals above what is considered the best. That means raising the unemployment goal to be higher than just achieving 0 percent unemployment in the traditional sense. That sense does not count large segments of the population as being unemployed. It simply defines them out of the labor force. It also does not count large segments of the labor force as being underemployed. Instead it defines being employed as simply having a job, regardless how part-time or how beneath one's capabilities.

Doing better than what was formerly considered the best is now only one kind of SOS. It may be less interesting in at least some ways because it may be simply a matter of definition, not a matter of actively pursuing well-placed subsidies, tax breaks, or new policies. One, however, does not solve the labor shortage problem simply by defining elderly people as being unemployed. One has to go further and talk about how to provide them with employment opportunities. We may, however, make a big difference if we start calling so-called retired people unemployed. Just calling them unemployed may stimulate them to become more interested in finding jobs, and it could stimulate potential employers into doing more to seek them out. The concept of being retired creates an image of somebody who is practically dead, senile, or decrepit in some sense. On the other hand, the concept of being unemployed (especially temporarily unemployed) creates an image of an able-bodied person who is willing and able to work if provided with appropriate opportunities.

In all the examples of doing better than the best by redefining *best*, we are talking about more than just definitions. How things are labeled does influence the behavior of the people who are so labeled or the doers of the activities. It also influences the behavior and attitudes of other people toward those activities. In the Hong Kong labor context, the super-optimum alternative involves the means for achieving the super-optimum goal of doing better than 0 percent unemployment. All the other alternatives focus on the tradeoff between importing labor and disrupting society or between not importing labor and losing additional prosperity.

Broader Implications

The Hong Kong labor problem illustrates labor problems throughout the world, not just Hong Kong. Every country has either a labor shortage or a labor surplus. Virtually no country considers its labor situation to be exactly in balance regarding supply and demand. The countries with a shortage are more dramatic—like Japan, South Korea, Taiwan, Singapore, Hong Kong, Malaysia, West Germany, and to some extent the United States. The countries with a labor surplus consist of most of the under-developed countries that are willing to export labor. This includes all of Central America, which exports labor to the United States, and northern South America, which does some exporting to Argentina and Chile but not much except in the sense of unskilled labor. The big exporting to the United States is, however, at both ends: unskilled labor from Mexico but a skilled brain drain from throughout the world, including China, India, eastern Europe, and western Europe. South Africa to a considerable extent operates as a labor importer from the front-line states, but strictly unskilled labor. It loses skilled labor to the rest of the world, including the United States and Canada. Israel is another example. It imports lots of unskilled labor from the West Bank but loses its skilled labor at the top to the United States. The Hong Kong problem is primarily one of the need for more labor at the bottom. It is not the kind of unskilled labor that works in the mines of South Africa but is the semi-skilled labor that works in the assembly plants throughout Asia, or at least throughout the Asian countries that have that kind of labor shortage.

The problem illustrates the need for having international economic communities like the European Economic Community (EEC) or the more recent Asian Economic Association of Nations (ASEAN). If such an international community functions properly, then the countries that have labor surpluses export to the countries that have labor shortages, and everybody is better off. There could also be interchanges between economic communities. There is—not in the sense that the Philippines is exporting labor to western Europe but in the sense that the Philippines is the largest source of labor in the Arab Middle East, and it sends a lot of people to Hong Kong, China, and the United States.

On a more methodological level, the Hong Kong labor problem illustrates better than any other problem the idea of multiple liberal groups and multiple conservative groups that do not get along with each other.

Another general principle that this example illustrates is the importance of how a policy problem is labeled. If the problem is referred to as the labor shortage problem of Hong Kong or Asia, then this tends to lead to a solution of importing more labor. If the problem is referred to as an immigration problem or an ethnic relations problem, then this tends to lead to a solution of avoiding the importing of more labor. The best way to refer to the problem is in such a way that one is pushed toward neither solution but instead toward thinking in terms of a super-optimum solution in which all sides can come out ahead of their best expectations. That might mean referring to the problem as the underemployment problem of Hong Kong or Asia. This label leads one to thinking about how to make more effective use of those willing and able people who are outside of the labor force and of those people inside the labor force who are not working up to their full potential.

SOME CONCLUSIONS

One point that was made by the participants in the seminars where materials like these were presented in China was that developing countries like China cannot afford the luxury of super-optimum solutions. Instead, they should perhaps be satisfied with something substantially less than super-optimum. That point sometimes implied that super-optimizing was too complicated except for people trained in computer science, mathematics, statistical analysis, operations research, and other sophisticated methodologies.

After the presentations, however, the consensus generally was that those methodologies are largely irrelevant. They can sometimes even be harmful if they cause paralysis or an overemphasis on unnecessary measurement and data. The prerequisites for super-optimizing analysis are basically to have (1) some knowledge of the key facts relevant to the problem, (2) an awareness of such political concepts as conservative and liberal, (3) an understanding of such decisional concepts as goals, alternatives, relations, tentative conclusions, and what-if analysis, and (4) some creativity in developing appropriate super-optimum solutions. This kind of creativity is made easier by having the first three of the four prerequisites. It is also made easier by having access to case studies like the ones previously discussed, so that one can learn from the experiences of other groups or individuals in trying to develop related super-optimum solutions.

The point about not being able to afford the luxury of super-optimum solutions may be the opposite of empirical and normative reality. The United States and other developed countries have less need for super-optimum solutions than developing countries do. The United States can probably go for a whole generation without developing any innovative ideas or coming close to solving any of its policy problems. If that happened, the United States would still have a high quality of life because it has such a well-developed cushion to fall back on. Developing countries, on the other hand, cannot afford to be satisfied with merely getting by. Doing so will put them further behind relative to other countries that are advancing rapidly, including countries that were formerly developing countries: Japan, Korea, Hong Kong, and Singapore.

In that context, super-optimum solutions are like free speech. Sometimes people in developing countries say they cannot afford free speech because it is too divisive. After they become more developed, then they can allow opposition parties and not have one-party systems with presidents for life. The reality is that they especially need to have free speech to stimulate creative ideas for solving their policy problems. Those problems are much more in need of solutions than the policy problems of well-developed countries.

A concrete example is the polio problem in Malawi. The country does not need Jonas Salk to invent a polio vaccine. The vaccine has already been invented. The country just needs to use it. Malawi does not use the vaccine adequately, not because it lacks the technology of having bottles of vaccine to pour into paper cups to give to the children to drink the vaccine but because Malawi happens to have a one-party state with a president for life who thinks that only doctors can give out vaccines, partly because he happens to be a doctor himself. People who speak out against that nonsense may find themselves in jail or worse. The problem is thus a free speech problem, not a technology problem.

On a higher level, the problem is an SOS problem. Polio could be greatly reduced or eliminated in Malawi by explaining to the headman in each village how to pour the vaccine from the bottles into the paper cups and how to have the children drink the vaccine. Doing so would probably mean the end of polio in Malawi, as it has meant the end of polio in the United States. President Hastings Banda could get the credit for having been responsible for ending what has been a horrible disease since the dawn of history in Central Africa. That should please the liberals, who are interested in better public health care. It should please the conservative president, who wants to be admired. More important, if this situation can be used for establishing a precedent about the importance of free speech in stimulating better public health care and better resolutions of other public policy problems, then the impact might extend to numerous ways in which the quality of life could be improved in the developing country of Malawi.

This is not an isolated example. Numerous examples have already been given in the previous case studies, and more examples could be given. What is needed are more applications of the basic ideas mentioned above, including the prerequisites for super-optimizing analysis. It is hoped that this chapter and the book of which it is a part will help stimulate those applications toward achieving super-optimum solutions to the public policy problems of developing and developed countries.[3]

NOTES

1. For further material on super-optimum solutions in which both liberals and conservatives come out ahead of their initial best expectations, see Susskind and Cruikshank (1987); Nagel (1990); and Nagel (1989).

2. This portion of the China food-prices problem is authored by Tong Daochi of the People's University of China. He also inspired the basic idea of applying super-optimizing to the food-pricing problem.

3. On policy problems in post-1945 China, see Harding (1987); Burns and Rosen (1986); and Major and Kane (1987).

REFERENCES

Burns, John, and Stanley Rosen, eds. 1986. *Policy Conflicts in Post-Mao China*. Armonk, N.Y.: M. E. Sharpe.

Harding, Harry. 1987. *China's Second Revolution: Reform After Mao*. Washington, D.C.: Brookings Institution.

Major, John, and Anthony Kane, eds. 1987. *China Briefing*. Boulder, Colo.: Westview Press.

Nagel, S. 1990. *Decision-Aiding Software: Skills, Obstacles, and Applications*. Hampshire, England: Macmillan.

———. 1989. "Super-Optimum Solutions in Public Controversies." *World Futures Quarterly* (Spring), 53–70.

Susskind, Lawrence, and Jeffrey Cruikshank. 1987. *Breaking the Impasse: Consensual Approaches to Resolving Disputes*. New York: Basic Books.

CHAPTER 8

Super-Optimum Solutions in Developmental Policy

King W. Chow

King W. Chow examines the problems of compensation for college faculty in China, as well as possible difficulties in Hong Kong after 1997 when Hong Kong will be restored to China. He describes the super-optimizing solutions approach as a viable strategy for policy analysts.

Education is a necessary underpinning for economic development and has not received its deserved attention. Chow notes that the average level of education in mainland China is less than five years and that almost one-quarter of one billion Chinese are illiterate. There is a lack of motivation for good performance, and it is difficult to recruit competent college faculty. Compared with the national average, college teachers seem to make sufficient income, but this is misleading because other residents can take part-time jobs or grow produce for themselves. There are fewer options available to faculty. Taxi drivers and waiters can make six times more per month than college faculty. Chow utilizes the Super-Optimum Solutions (SOS) approach to help identify the source of the problem and remove it. He describes changing the teacher/student ratio and, by so doing, making education accessible to students. Another suggestion is requiring tuition increases so as to permit higher salaries for faculty. He questions whether teacher work load would be unreasonably increased or whether tuition charges would unduly burden parents. SOS permits an unflinching assessment of the most negative consequences, which can then be reevaluated. Chow compares U.S. and Chinese teaching loads and argues that the compensation for increased work loads is justified and that the income promotes social prestige, as well as positive motivation.

Chow then turns to Hong Kong as it approaches the new status of being a Special Administrative Region in 1997, when it is projected that more civil servants and professionals will flee the country. He reports a survey of physicians, which suggests that only 1 percent of the 1,700 members of the Doctors' Association would be willing to remain in Hong Kong after 1997. Key problems for Hong Kong include civil servant pension guarantees and a stable administrative service. Chow points out that the residents' main goal is seeking protection rather than wanting to leave Hong Kong.

The possibility of the emigration of professionals means that those who remain will be under enormous pressure. He suggests that a "right of abode" (ROA) arrangement is better than any other possibilities because this means that the person may live in the country giving the right and could later apply for citizenship. The ROA would be valid for twenty or thirty years, thereby providing people with more access to freedom of choice of living. Hong Kong residents would be free to remain in Hong Kong but also free to leave when desiring to do so. A reward mechanism could also mandate that only high-performing civil servants would be entitled to receive the ROA.

Chow cautions that determining the SOS process differs from actually adopting its better-than-the-best solution. SOS deals with practical feasibility, and the adoption calls for political feasibility. Not everybody has the same goal. An educated population might challenge the government, and that may not be acceptable to the leadership. National analysis is, however, a necessary prerequisite to administrative progress and effectiveness.

The purpose of this chapter is to use two critical problems of development in Asia to illustrate the values and implications of Super-Optimum Solutions (SOS). The two cases selected are the policy problem of compensation for college teachers in China and the issue of incapacitation in the Hong Kong (HK) bureaucracy.

EDUCATION PROBLEM IN CHINA

Under Deng Xiaoping's leadership, China is caught up in the streams of development and modernization, striving to raise the standard of living of its population (1.08 billion). Since education is a major factor contributing to economic development, it should have received substantial attention from the communist leadership. Yet this has not been the case. Thus, many people can hardly write or speak proper Chinese; illiteracy has adversely affected the pace of economic development.

With the vast majority of the population being poorly educated, it is questionable whether China can achieve the goal of modernization. In light of the seriousness of the problem, one official of the National Education Commission recently admitted that the average years of education of the mainland Chinese is less than five years and that 0.22 billion Chinese are still illiterate.[1] Even Deng Xiaoping had to openly confess that the worst mistake committed by the government in the past ten years has been the lack of efforts to develop educational programs.[2]

To promote economic prosperity, the leadership must aim to enhance a better-educated work force. This, in turn, requires a more effective higher education system so as to produce more college graduates to satisfy the manpower needs of various development programs, particularly those for educating youngsters and illiterate adults. This mission, however, is almost impossible in the current situation for one simple reason: college teachers are not well paid, with the consequences that they lack the motivation to perform and that there are less able young men and women willing to become teachers.

Compensation for College Teachers

In China, a developing country governed by a Marxist-Leninist regime that subscribes to Mao Zedong's political philosophy, equitable pay has been a serious problem. As recent research has documented, the Communist leaders failed to establish a merit-based system for granting rewards to performers; therefore, state employees, particularly state cadres (civil servants), generally lacked the motivation to improve their performance, and their performance deficiencies created many social, economic, and political problems.[3]

Under Deng's leadership, reform measures were introduced in the 1980s for the purpose of allowing people to receive greater compensation for their efforts, for example, responsibility systems in farming and industrial plants and the relaxation of trading and commercial restrictions. Thus, some peasants could earn more than 10,000 yuan per year while blue-collar workers could easily make 500 yuan per month.[4]

These measures, however, have provided college teachers with little opportunities to earn additional income. As one Beijing professor pointed out, "Whereas some teachers may now serve as guest lecturers of training programs organized by adult-education institutes and earn some pocket money, these opportunities are hardly plentiful; most teachers could not find part-time jobs because of social pressure—after all, how could a teacher serve as, for example, an escort at a travel agency, even when he speaks good English?"[5] The primary source of income for teachers remains the regular salary.

Generally speaking, teachers are better off after the recent salary reform. In 1985, the "pragmatic" leadership adopted a new pay system, called Component-Salary System (*Jiegou gongji*).[6] Unlike the old one, the Currency-Salary System, under which a lump sum was paid to a teacher, the monthly salary under the Component-Salary System is composed of four elements, namely Basic Salary (*Jiben gongzi*), Job Position Salary (*Zhiwu gongzi*), Longevity Salary (*Gonglin gongzi*), and Incentive Salary (*Jiangli gongzi*). Specifically, all college teachers in a particular economic region receive a fixed amount as basic salary. For instance, teachers at Beijing, which is a Region Six city, receive 40 yuan; compensation is to be based on the ranking of individual officeholders. Thus, an associate professor at the pay step six, for example, receives a minimum of 100 yuan (i.e., 140 yuan, inclusive of basic salary), whereas a professor at the same pay step receives 130 yuan (i.e., 170 yuan, inclusive), a difference of 30 yuan (see table 8.1 for details). Compensation for each year's service is one-half yuan, with a maximum compensation of 20 yuan (i.e., forty years). A cash bonus is to be given to teachers on a monthly basis for performance cause—the average bonus, for example, at the People's University of China is 15 yuan.

Although the salary reform has resulted in a moderate increase in income,[7] academics are still unsatisfied. As of 1987, there were 385,000 college teachers (including approximately 10,000 professors and 60,000 associate professors).[8] Their average income was 1,409 yuan. Compared with the national average, as well as the income of state cadres (see table 8.2), college teachers are making a decent income. Yet the figures are grossly misleading, for two reasons. First, residents in urban areas can apply various strategies to increase their income, for example, by finding a part-time job. Peasants can now grow produce for personal consumption and public sales (with the latter bringing in a substantial increase in income, often at hundreds of yuan per year). Most employees in enterprises receive handsome bonuses, sometimes two to three times more than their regular pay.

Table 8.1
Pay Scale for Teaching Staff in Chinese Universities and Colleges

Pay Step/ Rank	Professor	Associate Professor	Lecturer	Teaching Assistant
Step 1	355	230	150	97
Step 1	300	205	140	89
Step 1	255	190	131	82
Step 2	230	180	122	76
Step 3	205	170	113	70
Step 4	190	160	105	N/A
Step 5	180	150	97	N/A
Step 6	170	140	N/A	N/A
Step 7	160	131	N/A	N/A
Step 8	N/A	122	N/A	N/A

Notes: All units are in yuan; the pay includes Basic Salary and Job Position Salary only.

Source: No. 9 Document issued by the Standing Committee of the Communist Party of China (1985).

Table 8.2
Average Incomes, 1981–87

Year	Average Income in China	Average Income of Teachers	Average Income of State Cadres
1981	772	716	815
1982	798	811	821
1983	826	836	923
1984	974	920	989
1985	1148	1166	1127
1986	1320	1330	1356
1987	1459	1409	1468

Notes: All unites are in yuan.
Source: *Statistics Year Book of the People's Republic of China* (1988), 191.

Second, many state cadres are corrupt and often abuse their authority for personal gains, in the form of money as well as gifts. Even noncorrupt cadres can assert influence, for example, to purchase quality products at below market price, itself a form of income increase, or to find a high-paying job for a relative. In short, many people earn much more than as reflected in the aforementioned figures, with the exception of college teachers.

Whereas college teachers are making an average of only 117 yuan per month, many other workers, such as waiters and taxi-drivers, are earning 600 to 700 yuan. In light of this substantial pay difference, many college graduates have chosen not to pursue a teaching career (or to receive graduate training in order to pursue an academic career). As one Beijing professor commented: "We academics could live on a shoe-string budget if the whole country is in depression, but we can't stand it when other people are making good money and we suffer for no particular reason, except that no one cares about our well-being; this reflects that our social status is very low and the consequence is inevitably that young men and women are unwilling to join our team."[9]

More important, many teachers are frustrated and lack motivation to perform. One Beijing teacher's comment best reflects the seriousness of the problem:

Many of my colleagues are regretful that they have chosen the teaching profession. To them, teaching yields neither extrinsic rewards nor psychological satisfaction for two reasons. Firstly, our pay is at such a low level that even a grade school graduate could easily make far more money than we do. And secondly, as money has become the primary yardstick for measuring one's worth, our salary is a disgrace to ourselves and our family. Many of my colleagues who are still single would remain single because girls these days have respect only for those who have earning powers. Could committed young men keep committing themselves to this profession? I don't think so. As a matter of fact, many teachers have already lost their interest in teaching. They just go into the classroom without much preparation; they just give easy grades in order to avoid student complaints; most of them just play cards, read novels, particularly kung-fu novels, or wander around doing nothing. This is sad, but it's the reality.[10]

The same informant also reported an interesting case: one renowned professor at Peking University, the equivalent of Harvard University in the Untied States, was so alarmed by the deteriorating quality of college education and the declining morale of teachers that he chose to express his frustration in 1989 by working as a part-time shoeshine man, moonlighting right at the main entrance of the university. Mockingly, his moonlighting job yielded an income of almost 500 yuan in just a week (150 yuan more than his monthly salary).

Seemingly, tertiary education will soon become a national crisis. As one professor in Guangzhou noted, "College teachers are smart people, and if grade school graduates could easily make 400 to 500 hundred yuan, we could do it too, if only we have not chosen teaching as our career; unless there is a substantial increase of our income, the quality of the tertiary programs will definitely drop while the quality of the teaching force will deteriorate as there are less able people joining and more capable teachers leaving the profession."[11]

What Is to Be Done

As table 8.3 reveals, whereas the leadership may wish to increase the salary for teachers, its capacity is limited: a budget deficit in the past years has almost become a norm, and there are few resources available for salary increases unless the leadership is willing to bear an even larger deficit. Moreover, since China has borrowed more than $40 billion from Western countries and since many loans are to mature in the early 1990s, while at the same time China's earning power has declined substantially after the Beijing military crackdown in 1989, the leadership is under tremendous financial stress. Thus, the probability that the leaders will grant handsome pay increases to college teachers is close to zero. The traditional approach to problem solving calls for compromise. From this perspective, a viable solution is to have the government squeeze out more money for college teachers, who then should settle for a small salary increase. This promise is better than the worst, but is hardly good enough. Yet, since China is under financial stress, this seems to be the best-available solution. However, with reference to Stuart S. Nagel's SOS approach, creative problem solvers shall aim to search for a better-than-the-best solution.[12] In this particular case, an SOS can be found if we identify the fundamental cause of the problem and remove it.

Table 8.3
Budget Surplus/Deficit, 1981–87

Year	Revenues	Outlays	Surplus/Deficit
1981	1089.6	1115.0	-25.5
1982	1124.0	1153.3	-29.3
1983	1249.0	1292.5	-43.5
1984	1501.9	1546.4	-44.5
1985	1866.4	1844.8	+21.6
1986	2260.3	2330.8	-70.6
1987	2346.6	2426.9	-80.3

Notes: All units are in 100 million yuan.
Source: *Statistics Year Book of the People's Republic of China* (1988), 762.

In China, college education is a precious commodity: students do not have to pay tuition; some can even receive state subsidy in form of a scholarship. More important, only a handful of high school graduates may enter college (see table 8.4). This means that the state is footing the bill of college education for a few students while many inspired young men and women cannot pursue college training, and that there is hardly any revenue from college students, as well as potential students. *These arrangements are the fundamental causes of the problem of inability to pay.*

From 1981 to 1987, as table 8.4 indicates, less than 5 percent of high school graduates were admitted to college. Moreover, as table 8.5 reveals, the teacher-student (T/S) ratio in universities and colleges—approximately one teacher to five students—is very low (as compared with the ratio of one to thirteen at the University of Hong Kong). Should the T/S ratio be changed to one to twenty, the total number of students would be increased from 1,959,000 to 7,700,000 (an addition of 5,741,000 students), and the number of first-year students admitted would be 1,925,000 (assuming that the intake of first-year students is one-fourth of the student population), that is, an increase of 1,308,000 students. Thus, whereas only 4.12 percent of high school graduates could enter college in 1987, a change in the T/S ratio could have resulted 12.86 percent of them attending college.

In addition, if each college student is required to pay a tuition in the amount of 240 yuan (per year), the revenue generated would amount to 1.85 billion yuan. If divided among the 385,000 teachers, each would receive 4,800 yuan per year, or 400 per month. Since the average income of teachers was 1,409 yuan per year

Table 8.4
Percentage of High School Graduates Admitted into College, 1981–87

Year	High School Graduates	Admitted into College	Percentage of Graduates Admitted
1981	1710.2	27.9	1.63
1982	1400.4	31.5	2.25
1983	1254.5	39.1	3.12
1984	1205.6	47.5	3.94
1985	1279.1	61.9	4.84
1986	1388.5	57.2	4.12
1987	1496.9	61.7	4.12

Notes: All units are in 10,000.

Source: Statistics Year Book of the People's Republic of China (1988), 874–77.

Table 8.5
Teacher-Student Ratio, 1981–87

Year	Number of College Teachers	Number of College Students	Teacher-Student Ratio
1981	25.0	127.9	1:5.12
1982	28.7	115.4	1:4.02
1983	30.3	120.7	1:3.98
1984	31.5	139.6	1:4.43
1985	34.4	170.3	1:4.95
1986	37.2	188.0	1:5.05
1987	38.5	195.9	1:5.09

Notes: All units are in 10,000.

Source: Statistics Year Book of the People's Republic of China (1988), 874–77.

in 1987 (117 per month), their (average) annual and monthly income could be increased to 6,209 yuan and 517 yuan, respectively.

As a super-optimum solution, these two arrangements together could effectively resolve the problem of the state's inability to give better pay to teachers and at the same time could generate more benefits for all parties concerned. First, a substantial increase in income for teachers is thus possible; second, there could be a drastic increase in the number of college students, thus granting more opportunities to inspired high school graduates and ensuring a more productive work force in the near future (a public good for all); and third, a relative contraction in government spending in tertiary education (in terms of average cost per student) could be realized, and thus the government could allocate the saved resources to other development policy areas.

Two questions deserve attention: Will work loads for teachers be increased after the change in T/S ratio? Will the tuition charge be a burden to parents? Regarding the latter, it is obvious that parents will have to chip in to support the college education of their children. In light of the national average income of 1,459 yuan per year in 1987 (see table 8.2), an increase to 240 yuan for tuition means that (on average) 16.4 percent of income will have to be consumed for college education. Yet, higher education is a quasi–public good, and parents themselves, in theory, should pay for at least part of it. Moreover, 16.4 percent of income for tuition is hardly unacceptable; parents in Western democracies have to spare a much larger chunk of their income to support their children. Furthermore, by chipping in, a better-educated work force would be enhanced, thus generating positive external effects—for example, better-managed service organizations, more-productive enterprises, and a more-efficient and more-effective state bureaucracy. Obviously, parents themselves would be beneficiaries of the new arrangement, that is, they would be better off.

Regarding work loads for teachers, these will have to increase. Nevertheless, teachers should accept the arrangement for three reasons. First, each college teacher is now required to teach only one course per year; a change in the T/S ratio from 1:5 to 1:20 probably resulting in an additional three courses, is still reasonable, at least as compared with the teaching loads in the United States. Second, since teachers would receive (on average) a 400 percent pay increase, the work load increase is well justified, particularly when they might have to do only two to three different preparations. And third, the substantial increase in income will promote their social prestige, a psychological benefit that is surely worth the efforts to teach more courses.

In sum, the proposed policy solution above could result in a better-than-the-best situation in which all parties concerned are better off. The following case will illustrate the same.

THE 1997 PHOBIA IN HONG KONG

Hong Kong (HK) has been a British colony since 1842. After 1997, however, China will resume her sovereignty over HK. Such a political arrangement was spelled out in the Joint Declaration released by China and the United Kingdom in 1984: specifically, HK will become a Special Administrative Region (SAR) and enjoy a "high degree of autonomy"; more important, the SAR will preserve the current capitalist system and life-style.[13] Despite the political guarantees of the Joint Declaration, many residents, particularly businessmen and professionals, have little confidence in the future of HK. The military crackdown in Beijing on June 4, 1989, further devastates the situation. It has produced even more serious stress in HK, leading to hundreds of thousands of people making up their minds to emigrate.[14] It is predicted, according to a recent HK government study, that at least one-half million people (close to 10 percent of the population) are likely to leave the territory before 1997.[15]

Incapacitation in the Hong Kong Bureaucracy

The 1997 phobia has created one critical issue, namely "brain drain" in both the public and the private sectors. Whereas the problem has adversely affected the community at large, its impact on the bureaucracy is particularly salient. For example, vacancy rates of government doctors and nurses in 1989 are 8 percent and 7 percent respectively.[16] The understaffing rate was 30 percent in 1989 at the Department of Rating and Evaluation [17] and 11 percent in the Urban Services Department[18]; the resignation rate was 11 percent at the Immigration Department in 1989[19] and 20 percent in the Department of Social Welfare.[20] (The overall wastage rate in the government was 5.9 percent in 1988 and 7.4 percent in 1989.[21])

Due to the manpower shortage problem, public executives find it difficult to maintain the quality of their programs. However, they can do little to alleviate the problem, since their hands are tied. For instance, whereas the government's compensation for senior officials is competitive,[22] it is not for lower-ranking civil servants,[23] thus making it difficult to fill vacated, as well as newly created, posts. The recruitment process is so lengthy that it takes, in exceptional cases, a minimum of eighteen weeks (from job application being received to the job being offered to the successful candidate), with an average of six to nine months.[24]

The Correctional Services Department (CSD) is a case in point. Whereas the staff shortage in 1989 was 23 percent (15 percent in 1988), the overall staff wastage in CSD was about 13 percent in 1988.[25] An inadequate supply of new blood, coupled with depletion of experienced staff, has compelled the management to undertake various measures to avoid incapacitation, including (1) asking its staff to defer their leave, (2) cutting down training time, and (3) lowering entry qualification and requirements.[26]

Despite these efforts, several incidents have shown that incapacitation still exists. For instance, CSD staff were unable to maintain order at Vietnamese refugee camps—conflicts among various Vietnamese factions repeatedly led to bloodshed, and CSD staff, including senior officials, were brutalized.[27] CSD staff were also unable to stop fights among inmates in detention centers, a problem that was extremely rare in HK prisons until recently.

More important, due to the aforementioned measures taken to avoid incapacitation, CSD staff are under excessive stress—heavier work loads, less time off, less family and social life, and increasing job pressures. As a result, more staff are considering resignation or early retirement. Obviously, CSD is trapped in a vicious circle: as more CSD staff leave the service, the incapacitation problem will escalate, and thus the management must take remedial actions, which would result in further wastage.

The CSD situation reveals the serious problem of incapacitation; unfortunately, it is hardly atypical. Executives in other agencies also find the problem of incapacitation difficult to deal with. Yet, they can do little because of the 1997 phobia. The situation in government hospitals best reflects the problem. A recent survey conducted by the Hong Kong Government Doctors' Association indicates that among the association's 1,700 members, only seventeen doctors (1 percent) plan to stay in HK after 1997; 663 (39 percent) had already applied for immigration, and the other 1,020 doctors (60 percent) are planning on leaving.[28] With the drainage of medical doctors, Tuen Mun Hospital, the largest in HK, can make only 344 beds available to patients, although the full capacity is 1,606 beds.[29]

As more civil servants are lacking confidence in the political future of HK and thus are planning on emigration or are joining the private sector (to earn more money and therefore be in a better financial position to apply for immigration to such countries as Canada and Australia by means of investment), the brain drain problem in the bureaucracy will intensify, as will the incapacitation problem. How can the HK government resolve its incapacitation problem? Recent research on HK public administration has yielded findings relevant to this question. For example, Scott's analysis of the changes in the policy-making environment indicates that the government should increase "investment of more resources in the policy-making system in order to make it more responsive to, and congruent with, the turbulent environment.[30] Cheek-Milby's study of personnel management issues suggests that the government needs to address such problems as civil servant pension guarantees and fear of political manipulation of the civil service, so as to maintain "a stable administration during and beyond the transition.[31] Lui's review of civil servant values documents the need to advance a new ethic for the civil service.[32] And Clark's examination of ecological changes and the government's capacity to cope with those changes reveals that the government must develop an agenda for administrative change.[33]

The main thrust of this literature has been to underscore the necessity of reform (be it with reference to policy making, personnel management, or value development). Yet, can administrative reform help to restore civil servants' confidence in HK? None of the current research reports about HK furnish a basis for addressing this critical question.

What Is to Be Done?

The governments in Britain, China, and HK have reiterated that the Joint Declaration will be honored. HK residents, however, are still fearful. Thus, the problem of brain drain is likely to prevail. The traditional approach to problem solving calls for bargaining. Thus, from this perspective, possible viable solutions are pay increase and enrichment of perks for civil servants, increase of government spending to ensure attractiveness of promotion prospects, and legalization of guarantee of pension for civil servants. The HK government has adopted all these measures; unfortunately, the increasing numbers of resignations and applications to emigrate have shown that all these better-than-nothing solutions are ineffective.

To search for an SOS, we must identify the fundamental cause(s) of a problem. In this case, the 1997 phobia is the cause of incapacitation. Moreover, the ultimate causes of the phobia are that due to the military crackdown in Beijing, the current leadership has lost its credibility and that HK residents are afraid they would have nowhere to go to if China does not honor the Joint Declaration. There is nothing one can do at this time to remove the first cause because it will take a long time for the Beijing leadership to prove its trustworthiness.

Regarding the second cause, the truth of the matter is that most residents do not want to leave HK. They are just seeking protection. Without an emergency exit, the risk of staying in HK is far too great for any reasonable person to bear. Seemingly, if residents have the right of abode in other countries, and thus could take off when necessary, they would be willing to stay.

In light of this understanding, some HK residents immediately pressed for British citizenship after the June 4 massacre. Their objective was to secure citizenship for 3.25 million residents who are being classified as citizens of British Dependent Territories but who had their right to reside in Britain deprived in 1962 after the UK government amended its immigration law.

The drive to secure UK passports, however, was bound to be unsuccessful because the UK government cannot afford to take the high risk of accepting one to two million poor people from HK. Any reasonable person can speculate that after 3.25 million HK residents receive the British passport, the rich and the professionals may still emigrate to such other countries as Canada, the United States, and Australia, whereas those who actually emigrate to the UK are likely to be the ones who cannot go elsewhere, namely the poor, blue-collar workers, non–English speaking people, and any others who are likely to be on welfare. Recent developments in London indeed reveal that the UK government plans to give British passports to only 225,000 HK residents, a figure much lower than HK people are asking for.

The passport arrangement is surely better than the other solutions mentioned. Yet, it is likely to be ineffective for three reasons. First, with only 3.75 percent of the population holding the key to the exit door, the stabilizing effect will be limited when another 400,000 to 500,000 are leaving. Second, the quality of life in Britain is unattractive to many HK residents, whose disposition is, when necessary, to emigrate to the United States, Canada, or Australia. Thus, the British citizenship cannot effectively induce HK residents to take the risk of having their civil rights deprived by the SAR government after 1997 and then live in Britain after they are compelled to retreat. And third, since passport holders may leave at any time, the probability of having them rushing to Britain (even before 1997) when another crisis emerges—for example, another massacre in Beijing or a massive exodus in HK—is high. Obviously, the effectiveness of the British passport arrangement as a solution is questionable. More important, this policy solution fails to make all parties concerned better off. For example, whereas the Chinese leadership is vitally concerned with stability and prosperity in HK, it finds this arrangement unacceptable because it believes that the UK government is trying to ensure influence in HK after 1997. Civil servants are also unhappy because, under the proposed plan, only 12,500 civil servants—that is, 7 percent of the service (the current strength of the civil service is 180,000-plus)—could receive British passports. Even members of Parliament in the United Kingdom are apprehensive about the possible influx of 225,000 people from HK, thus creating many social problems, particularly racial conflicts.

The demerits of the proposed British passport arrangement reveal four pitfalls. First, granting passports may actually contribute to the exodus. Second, having a small number of HK residents holding the key to the exit door is unlikely to generate a stabilizing effect. Third, foreign passport arrangements would alienate the Beijing leadership, which has little interest in having HK internationalized (i.e., HK residents being foreigners). And fourth, the interests of countries granting passports may be adversely affected by HK residents' exodus.

All these imply that a conditional right of abode (CROA) arrangement is a better-than-the-best solution. CROA is similar to the right of entry, with the exception that the person possessing such a right may reside permanently in the country granting the right and may subsequently apply for citizenship, if determined by the country concerned to be necessary. Moreover, CROA would be granted to qualified HK residents in the form of a visa, and the visa shall be valid for twenty to thirty years from its issuance date. With CROA, HK residents will be able to retreat to, for example, the United States for a temporary stay, thus protecting themselves from any political suppression or exploitation. With such a guarantee, anxious HK residents will be willing to hang around to contribute to the economic prosperity and political stability in the territory.

The CROA arrangement can effectively resolve the brain drain problem and, thus, incapacitation in the bureaucracy because, first, a much larger portion of the population—up to two million if all Western democracies participate in this safety network scheme—holding the key to the exit door can become a critical mass generating a stabilizing effect and, second, since China cannot afford to have one-fourth of the HK population leave, HK residents may have far greater confidence in their ability to bargain with the Beijing leadership when it tries to break its promises spelled out in the Joint Declaration.

More important, the CROA scheme ensures that everybody is better off. First, many HK residents, who enjoy the current life-style and career prospects, particularly the professionals and businessmen, may remain in HK, and when necessary, they can retreat to countries of their preference for a temporary stay. Although other residents may not be in possession of CROA, they can still feel more secured because the probability of having stability and prosperity in HK after 1997 is greater.

Second, due to the CROA restrictions that permit HK residents to apply for permanent residence in a particular country *only* when the political condition in HK justifies the application, foreign countries would have to worry little about the possible influx of HK people, which is likely if they are in possession of passports of those countries.

Third, whereas political oppression after 1997 might compel holders of CROA to leave, the receiving countries may claim the credit for taking humane actions to help the needy, an intangible benefit all governments in Western democracies aim to acquire.

Fourth, with the CROA scheme in place, the Beijing leadership will feel the pressure and will be compelled to be more cautious in making policies that might destabilize the HK situation. As such, the restoration of HK residents' confidence is more likely.

Fifth, although the scheme would contribute to the promotion of political stability and economy prosperity in HK, and in turn to the economic development in China, the scheme will hardly result in the internationalization of HK, which, to the Beijing leadership, is an act of challenge to the sovereignty of China.

And sixth, the HK government may have the incapacitation problem effectively resolved and even have the productivity of the bureaucracy improved. For example, should the HK government press Britain to adopt the CROA proposal (and to push for an international safety network scheme in order to secure CROA for people in the private sector), the originally proposed 225,000 passports can then be turned into CROA and be given to civil servants, with a prescribed condition that only well-performing civil servants are qualified to receive CROA. The likely consequences are that more talented people will join the civil service, and incumbents will be induced to perform; both would help to ensure efficient operation of the bureaucracy and effective delivery of services to the public.

All in all, the CROA scheme is a super-optimum solution, which will generate more benefits to all.

DISCUSSION

The two cases discussed above demonstrate that in addition to those being discussed by Stuart Nagel, one viable strategy for policy analysts to come up with an SOS is to direct their efforts to identify the fundamental cause of a policy problem and the possible ways of removing it. More important, the two cases reveal that SOSs are possible when policy analysts adopt the SOS paradigm, a worldview based on an optimistic assumption about the possibility of finding better-than-the-best solutions and on a moral prescription that analysts should aim to develop policy solutions that make all parties concerned better off.

This observation merits serious attention from policy analysts concerned with metapolicy. Since metapolicy is policy about making policies, it is composed of major guidelines for policy action. Fundamental to the concept of metapolicy-making is that policymakers are to ''establish doctrines and methods . . . for dealing with uncertainty'' and ''other substantive and methodological instructions for policy-making.''[34] Yet, what are those doctrines and methods? If the findings presented here, as well as the others in this book, are convincing, one may feel comfortable to entertain the idea that SOS as a paradigm (at the policy level) and as a problem-solving method (at the program level) may well be the metapolicy in the 1990s, with the ''doctrine'' prescribing that ''he who analyzes is obliged to propose how to benefit all'' and with the method (strategy) for identifying SOS as presented here. Future research to substantiate or repudiate this argument is essential to our quest for a metapolicy.

On the practical side, one note of caution is in order: formulating an SOS is different from having it adopted. The former involves engineering feasibility, whereas the latter concerns political feasibility.

The underlying assumptions of the analysis of the two cases here are that, first, all parties concerned are rational actors in that they are consistent in the pursuit of adopted goals and that they consistently choose the most *effective* means to accomplish stated ends. Second, they are also vitally concerned with the policy problems examined. It follows from these assumptions that the parties involved in the cases *may* consider themselves players in a non–zero-sum game pursuing the greatest possible benefits for all. Thus, it is further assumed that SOS would be adopted.

In reality, these assumptions may be invalid: players may not share the same objective and/or consider themselves the players in a positive-sum game, and thus they may not accept the goal of making everyone better off; players may be nonrational, or even irrational, actors. For example, whereas Deng Xiaoping and his followers may wish to enhance a more productive work force, they may believe that political indoctrination is a more effective strategy to improve productivity, although such past experiences as the Great-Leap Forward Movement (1958–59) and the cultural revolution (1966–76) have indicated that indoctrination may merely create more problems than it can resolve. Besides, they may also perceive that a better-educated population is more likely to challenge their policies and their authority. If so, the probability of having the proposed SOS adopted by them is close to zero. By the same token, if key policymakers (mostly British) in HK are not concerned with political stability after 1997, they would have little interest in pressing for an international safety network scheme, which, to them, would generate little benefits but would consume much of their time and resources. In this light, although the engineering feasibility of the two SOSs presented here is affirmative, the political feasibility is not.

Seemingly, the necessary conditions for coming up with a technically and politically feasible SOS are that participants must be vitally concerned with the same policy and that they must consider the game a positive-sum game. This suggestion is congruent with Bozeman's assertion: ''The conceptual frameworks and cognitive styles which policymakers bring to decision processes determined the usefulness of analytically-based policy analysis."[35] Moreover, this understanding is in line with Webber's argument: "In a democratic policy process, the political feasibility of a proposed policy alternative is paramount. While the technical soundness of a strategy proposed to solve a controversial policy problem should be a necessary condition for its adoption, policy alternatives that do not have widespread political support are not likely to be adopted.[36]

Thus, policy analysts should recognize that an SOS is possible *if and only if* the aforementioned necessary conditions are present. For example, when this proposition above is applied in the American context to diagnose policy problems, one may comfortably predict that, first, in light of the national concern for the drug problem in the United States, this problem is amenable to SOS and that second, in view of the conflict of values involved in the making of gun-control policy, the formulation and adoption of SOS here will be impossible unless participants' values or perceptions of the nature of the game have changed.

The proposition about the necessary conditions for the formulation and adoption of an SOS deserves serious research attention. Since the causal relationship between the necessary condition and its corresponding events is deterministic, taking the form of "if X, then Y is possible," or "if not X, then not Y," propositions about the possibility of an event's occurrence are essential to theory building. After all, propositions about the *possibility* of an event's occurrence, as compared with propositions about *profitability*, tend to have greater explanatory and predictive powers.

As Ingraham has criticized agencies, when confronting policy problems "turn to similar agencies, states to other states, and nations to other nations in the common search for problem solution. What is missing is a serious effort to determine the exact nature of the problem and its causes, the potential range of solutions, and the most appropriate strategy for achieving desired outcomes. Also notably absent is a theory, or sets of theories, the purpose of which is to guide policy design."[37] Seemingly, if policy analysts are to avoid the pitfalls underscored by Ingraham, they need to systematically examine the nature of different policy problems and to identify the necessary conditions for an SOS for those policy problems. These pursuits will facilitate both problem solving and the formulation of "a theory, or sets of theories."

NOTES

An earlier draft of this chapter was presented at the 1990 conference of the American Society for Public Administration. The author wishes to thank Professor Stuart S. Nagel for his helpful comments on the early draft and the Center for Hong Kong Studies of the Chinese University of Hong Kong for its financial support for this research project.

1. See "Li Responding to Questions about Education," *Renmin Ribao (People's Republic Daily)*, March 25, 1990, 1.

2. See "The Worst Error Is Underdevelopment of Education," *Renmin Ribao*, March 24, 1990, 1.

3. See, for example, King W. Chow: "The Management of Chinese Cadre Resources: Reforms, Problems, and Implications of Pay Administration (1949–1987)," *Public Budgeting and Financial Management* 1, no. 1 (1989): 67–98; "The Management of Chinese Cadre Resources: Job Evaluation and Position Classification (1949–1987)," *Issues and Studies* 24, no. 8 (1986): 11–33; "The Management of Chinese Cadre Resources: The Politics of Performance Appraisal (1949–1984)," *International Review of Administrative Sciences* 54, no. 3 (1988): 359–78; and "Equity and Cadre Job Performance: Causation and Implications," *Issues and Studies* 23, no. 9 (1987): 58–71.

4. The official exchange rate on March 13, 1990, was approximately 474 yuan to 100 U.S. dollars, or one yuan to exactly 21.10 cents.

5. Interview with a Beijing professor in May 1989.

6. For a detailed discussion of the reform, see Chow, "Chinese Cadre Resources: Reforms."

7. There are no statistics showing the amount of pay increase. Nevertheless, according to five Beijing academics interviewed by this researcher in July 1987, the average increase was almost 20 percent.

8. *The 1988 People's Republic of China Year Book* (Beijing: New China Publishing Co., 1988), 455.

9. Interview with a Beijing professor who visited Hong Kong in January 1990; the interview was conducted on January 23, 1990.

10. Interview with a Beijing teacher, who visited Hong Kong in the spring of 1990; the interview was conducted on March 2, 1990.

11. Interview conducted in Guangzhou on February 17, 1990.

12. See Nagel's Introduction in this book.

13. For the text and annex of the Joint Declaration, see Norman Miners, *The Government and Politics of Hong Kong*, 4th ed. (Hong Kong: Oxford University Press, 1986). For scholarly analyses of the issues of the Joint Declaration, see, for example, Ian Scott, "Policy Making in a Turbulent Environment: The Case of Hong Kong," *International Review of Administrative Sciences* 52, no. 4 (1986): 447–69, and *Political Change and the Crisis of Legitimacy in Hong Kong* (Hong Kong: Oxford University Press, 1989).

14. For example, 8,869 persons applied to emigrate to Australia in the latter part of the year, whereas only 3,221 applied in the same period in 1988 ("Emigration Application to Australia Almost Treble," *South China Morning Post*, February 28, 1990, 1); 25,000 persons also applied to emigrate to Singapore in the same period, and 16,000 applications have been approved ("16,000 Families Set to Go," *South China Morning Post*, February 24, 1990).

15. For details, see "Brain Drains," *AmCham, the Journal of the American Chamber of Commerce in Hong Kong*, December 1989, 29–37.

16. Dennis Wong, "Staff Shortage Threatens Care Services: Doctor," *Hong Kong Standard*, December 29, 1989.

17. Wilson Wong, "Staff Policy Hit by Brain Drain," *Hong Kong Standard*, October 11, 1989.

18. Jennifer Cooke, "Four-point Program to Tackle Staff Wastage," *South China Morning Post*, October 13, 1989.

19. "Immigration Bid for Staff after Resignations," *Hong Kong Standard*, May 27, 1989.

20. Leung Sze-man "Welfare Heading for Crisis over Manpower," *Hong Kong Standard*, November 17, 1989.

21. The current strength of the Hong Kong civil service is 180,000 plus. For details of wastage rate, see Yue Sin-yue, "Localization Beats Wastage," *Hong Kong Standard*, December 16, 1989.

22. Jessie Yim, "The Growing Challenge of Maintaining a Civil Service," *Hong Kong Standard*, November 4, 1989.

23. Ibid. See also "Increasing Civil Servant Workload Worst Possible Strategy," *South China Morning Post*, November 22, 1989.

24. Vivian Tse, "Government Hiring Process Deters Applicants," *Hong Kong Standard*, November 4, 1989.

25. Lina Ma, "Alarming Staff Wastage a Persistent Problem for the Correctional Services," *Hong Kong Standard*, June 19, 1989, 11.

26. Ibid.

27. For reports, see, for example, "Officers Attacked by Boat People," *South China Morning Post*, November 7, 1989, 1.

28. For details, see "Poll Warns of Doctors Mass Exodus," *South China Morning Post*, January 26, 1990.

29. Mary Ann Bennitez, "Shortage of Staff Hits New Hospital," *South China Morning Post*, March 9, 1990.

30. Scott, "Policy Making in a Turbulent Environment," 447.

31. Kathleen Cheek-Milby, "Changing Civil Servants' Values," in Ian Scott and John P. Burns, eds., *The Hong Kong Civil Service and Its Future* (Hong Kong: Oxford University Press, 1988), 123.

32. Terry T. Lui, "Changing Civil Servants' Values," in Scott and Burns, *The Hong Kong Civil Service*, 131–66.

33. David Clark, "Towards a More Open Administration," in Scott and Burns, *The Hong Kong Civil Service*, 192.

34. Gerald W. Johnson and John G. Heilman, "Metapolicy Transition and Policy Implementation: New Federalism and Privatization," *Public Administration Review* 47, no. 6 (1987): 471.

35. Barry Bozeman, "The Credibility of Policy Analysis: Between Method and Use," *Policy Studies Journal* 14, no. 4 (1986): 527.

36. David J. Webber, "Analyzing Political Feasibility: Political Scientists' Unique Contribution to Policy Analysis," *Policy Studies Journal* 14, no. 4 (1986): 545.

37. Patricia W. Ingraham, "Toward More Systematic Consideration of Policy Design," *Policy Studies Journal* 15, no. 4 (1987): 613.

PART IV

Diverse Evaluations

CHAPTER 9

An Insider's Perspective

Xia Shuzhang

Xia Shuzhang examines the development of public administration within the People's Republic of China. Although it is one of the oldest professions, the field as a whole suffered from its dissolution for many critical years. Public administration associations were organized in the 1940s, yet in the 1950s, public administration instruction was stopped and did not resume again for almost thirty years. The author is one of the key voices in pressing for the relevance and necessity of public administration education. In 1982, political science courses began again at Fudan University. Public administration was also taught. A major textbook on public administration, with Professor Xia as the editor-in-chief, was published in 1985.

Xia points with pleasure to the increasing number of seminars and symposia held nationwide, as well as the steady development of public administration associations. What is extremely interesting is the greater breadth and range of programs in which public administration is taught. Over 100 new volumes have appeared dealing with public administration.

Xia points to the need to disseminate and improve. These are possibly conflicting trends. One wants to broaden knowledge but at the same time recognize the limits of further broadening without a deepening in research and publication. The goal is the establishment of socialist public administration within the Chines framework.

He also points to the great necessity for trained public administrators, given the enormous range of formal structures of cities, counties, towns, villages, and provinces. Even if one was to think of only one trained public administrator for each governmental unit, the numbers would be legion. In addition to training, there is also the need for a high quality of training, as well as for the support and development of teaching and research personnel. In the rebuilding of the discipline, complete courses need to be set up. As Xia puts it, "This is an academic field to be reclaimed and carefully cultivated."

There is also a need for an understanding of what can be learned from other countries and what must be adapted to the Chinese experience. Although there has to be a reverence for the past, there must also be a recognition of the importance of adjusting current thinking to build on traditions. Xia recognizes the importance of linking many disciplines within public administration and is hopeful that resources can be used intelligently to improve public administration and administrative reform.

Public administration and policy studies are, relatively speaking, young applied sciences in the PRC. Under the present circumstances, it is very important and necessary to pay more attention to the study of administrative science and its development. As an "old soldier" in this field for more than half a century, and believing that one is never too old to learn, I would like to express some ideas about it.

A BRIEF HISTORICAL REVIEW

Public administration is one of the oldest professions, especially in China. A subject entitled "Public Administration" appeared in Europe in the latter part of the nineteenth century, yet it mainly covered administrative law, not public administration in its actual sense. It was in the 1920s that this became a widely accepted subject, to be included in the formal curriculum, and the subject was established in the United States only a little more than sixty years ago, since 1926–27 or so. Public administration is very closely related to administrative law, but as a subject public administration was first classified with political science. During and after World War II, the rise of managerial science enriched and strengthened the research work in public administration. Since then, a tendency toward cross-discipline has become obvious.

In old China, the nature of society had step by step become semicolonial and semifeudal since the Opium War in 1840. Afterward, the international powers colluded with Chinese warlords to divide China into their spheres of influence, and the sovereign state was split up. By the end of the Qing Dynasty, the old examination system (to recruit government officials) was abolished, as China started to learn from the West. The educational system and academic viewpoints were influenced by people in power and by scholars who had studied abroad. In most cases, these people just copied foreign ways mechanically. Further and independent study to combine theory with practice was not stressed, which is understandable in that period. Before the anti-Japanese war, public administration and administrative law were taught in universities and colleges. In wartime, the Chinese Public Administration Association was organized in 1943, whose members were mainly higher officials of the Guomindang government. A year later, another Chinese

Public Administration Association was established, whose members were mainly scholars and professors. After the liberation of the mainland, a "Chinese Public Administration Association was reestablished in Taiwan (actually, it is a provincial organization) in 1954. It seems that there are no longer two associations and that the teaching and research of public administration is going on in Taiwan.

Before the PRC was formally founded, in the revolutionary bases and liberated areas, the Communist Party of China had paid much attention to cadres' training, setting up some departments or divisions of public administration in revolutionary schools at different levels. But as the regular systems of education had not been established, it was difficult to carry on a concentrated and systematic study of pubic administration, as now. After the PRC was founded, when the curriculum reform began in 1952, the teaching of public administration was stopped. We thought it was a temporary discontinuity, but it was not continued until the 1980s. We lost a lot of time.

A GENERAL ANALYSIS OF THE PRESENT SITUATION

In the early stage of liberation, due to the curriculum reform in the institutions of higher learning, the subject of public administration was changed into "Administrative Organization and Management." The students were very much interested in this course for its practical nature. It was a regrettable fact that this subject was cancelled from the curriculum for thirty years or so, as mentioned above. Frankly speaking, this was disadvantageous to discipline construction, cadre training, and administrative reform.

To meet the need of reform, I wrote an article entitled "Now It Is Time to Place the Study of Public Administration on the Agenda," which was published in the *People's Daily*, page 5, on January 29, 1982, appealling to the readers to support the study of public administration. In the same year, the Chinese Political Science Association entrusted Fudan University in Shanghai to run a short-term class on political science. Public administration was taught in the class and attracted quite a few students. Seven of them took part in writing a textbook on public administration, for which I was the editor-in-chief and which was published by Shanxi Publishing House in 1985. It is supposed to be one of the earlier attempts to promote the study of public administration in the PRC.

The development of public administration now is delightful. Many seminars and symposia are held nationwide. The earlier and higher-ranking symposia were sponsored by the General Office of Administration of the State Council and Ministry of Labor and Personnel Administration, held in Jiling City, Jiling Province, in 1984, and by the Chinese Political Science Association and the Chinese Law Association, held in Tianjing in the same year. Public administration associations, not only national, but also provincial and municipal, were set up one after another. These formed a very good mass foundation for the development of public administration.

Public administration has developed more and more specialties, all with students enrolled at various levels, including junior colleges undergraduate colleges and universities, college correspondence courses, night school (college level), college through broadcasting and television ("open university"), higher education through self-study examination, post-graduate programs with M.P.A. degrees, and so on.

Training programs and research institutes are developing rapidly. The National School of Public Administration is being developed, while many provincial and municipal schools of public administration are already operating. In different kinds of cadre and party schools, all the students must study public administration as a course.

Many textbooks and reference books have been published. In the past five to six years, the total number of these publications, including handbooks and dictionaries, is over one hundred volumes, by rough estimate.

Varieties of professional periodicals, magazines, and journals can be used for reference. Many discussions, articles, and other information concerning public administration can be read in the newspapers from time to time. International exchange programs or joint projects have begun, including international conferences and mutual visits between scholars and administrators. And the Chinese Public Administration Society was approved as "Chinese National Section" by the IIAS (International Institute of Administrative Sciences).

It is fair to say that great progress has been made in the study of public administration in the PRC. It is still our main task to make the science of public administration more popularized. But at the same time, to popularize and to improve cannot be sharply separated. This is why I made an appeal for improving the study of public administration, which is in the preface to the book *New Approaches to Public Administration*, which was printed in Hubei Province in January 1988. The key point in improving the study of public administration is to work harder in combining theory with practice so as to build up socialist public administration with Chinese characteristics to serve the administrative reform.

A PRELIMINARY OUTLOOK

Just like the socialist modernization, the development of public administration is quite hopeful and optimistic in the light of the contemporary situation. We can see the future, and at least we have very good reasons to make the following preliminary estimates.

First, the modernization of public administration is necessary, and the demand is already shown in the process of reform. The number of people who need the education or training of pubic administration is very large in the PRC, a big country with a large population. Approximately, there are 450 formal cities, 2,000 counties, and tens of thousands of towns and villages, besides the central (national) and provincial governmental units. Trying to supply each unit with one qualified, well-trained public servant will be a tremendous job, to say nothing of the needed administrators in nongovernmental enterprises, who number in the millions.

Second, closely following the new development of the socialist modernization and the practice of reform and open policy, the need for administrators with higher-quality and better training is rapidly growing. It is not only a matter of quantity but also a matter of quality. That is to say, the level of teaching and research must be raised. "When the river rises, the boat floats high," as the old saying goes. As Mao Zedong once said: "If popularization remains at the same level forever, . . . will not the educators and those being educated be six of one and half a dozen of the other? What would be the sense of such popularization?" (*Selected Works of Mao Tse-Tung*, Volume III, p. 83) This is also true.

Third, well-educated teaching and research personnel are therefore important. The matter of personnel is directly related to satisfying the need for popularizing and improving public administration education or training. Because of the high applicability of the science of public administration, theory must be combined with practice, and the teaching and research personnel must be well educated both in theory and in practice. When either is too weak, it must be made strong. Both theory and practice are constantly changing. Renewing the ideas and experiences is always needed.

Fourth, the construction of series of teaching materials must be well planned. Public administration as a specialty needs to offer a complete set of courses. In some districts or unit, this kind of work has begun. But it is still worthwhile to promote concentrated research. We will take the responsibility of not doing it rashly. "Haste makes waste" is believable. To waste manpower, material resources, time, and money is against the principle of efficiency, which is one of the important principles in modern administration or management.

Finally, since we start our research work late in the field of public administration, we have to make a double effort to do it well. There are many things to be done, not only the fundamental ones but also the exploitative and special ones. For example, from the top to the bottom (especially the city) level, in various departments (such as defense, foreign affairs, education, health, and transportation), in special economic zones, in special administrative zones ("one nation, two systems"), and inside administration, there are many subjects to be studied (such as organization, personnel, planning, leadership, and decision making). In short, this is an academic field to be reclaimed and carefully cultivated in the PRC. It is an elaborate job, which must be carefully prepared and finished.

SEVERAL ISSUES OF THE STUDY OF PUBLIC ADMINISTRATION AND POLICY STUDIES IN THE PRC

In the study of public administration, there are many problems and issues, which need much discussion. Here are just some important examples. The most important aim is to build socialist public administration with Chinese characteristics. The examples center on this aim.

First, we must take a correct attitude toward the experiences of foreign countries and other areas. At the very beginning, simply or entirely introducing the situation from abroad is unavoidable. Ordinarily, we should learn all good things from other countries and districts, regardless of whether they are big or small, rich or poor, strong or weak, far or near, old or new. But one thing must be borne in mind as a basic principle: whatever we learn, we must see if it is suitable to China and not learn it mechanically, not "swallow raw or whole" or "cut the feet to fit the shoes." That is to say, we must adopt the strong points and give up the shortcomings or try to digest, to overcome our weakness, by acquiring others' strong points, not copy others and make ourselves look foolish. To know China well is essentially important.

Second, we need to learn from the past. China has a long history. It is a matter of the ability to select and not to stick to outmoded ways and things, not to revive old ways blindly. We know that many foreign scholars are doing research work on managerial thoughts in ancient China, the book *Sun Zi Bing Fa* is regarded as the earliest classical work on management or administration. This can enlighten us on the subject, but it does not mean that we should continue on the beaten track, for we are now living in modern China.

Third, we must be very clear in mind that socialism and capitalism are fundamentally different in nature. When we take some successful experiences for reference, we must know that it is just for the benefit of our socialist construction, whether it concerns method, technique, theory, or purpose. Our real and sole purpose is to serve the people.

Fourth, as for science and experience, we respect the former. Scientific socialism requires doing and thinking everything in a scientific way, liberating ourselves entirely from backwardness. In the study of public administration, we need the scientific world outlook and methodology—dialectical materialism and historical materialism. For experiences, we should conduct scientific analysis. Only scientific experiences are useful. Empiricism is harmful.

Fifth, as we emphasized again and again, combining theory with practice is especially important in the study of public administration. Neither one must be overemphasized to the neglect of the other. We must seek truth from facts; that is to say, the research work must be done in a practical way in order to get the best results—not building castles in the air, not drawing a cake to satisfy one's hunger, not fighting only on paper (prating). The bridge between theory and practice is to ponder actively and creatively. To meet with this requirement, one must understand very well both the theoretical side and the practical side, and one needs all the practical departments for support. We expect to put theory and practice together just like milk and water, not oil and water.

Sixth, public administration is not a narrow and isolated course. It is closely related to many disciplines: political science, psychology, economics, public finance, law (especially administrative law), sociology, management, and science of leadership. In doing research work on public administration, the more knowledge one has, the better.

The issues worth discussing are various. It is not necessary to list all of them. We hope that those who are interested in this field will make joint efforts in helping this course of instruction to grow and develop.

As we pointed out in the beginning, this is a new discipline in the PRC. Many of the colleagues in this field have transferred from other fields, such as philosophy, history, or literature. Even those who are "veterans" are also new to socialist public administration with Chinese characteristics. Therefore, the "starting point" for everyone, old or young, is roughly the same. We need mutual encouragement and good cooperation to coordinate with one another. In doing research work, we had better make use of collective wisdom in order to avoid doing research separately at a low level. Let's try to do our best and use the limited resources in a clever way to make more and better contributions to the science of public administration and contemporary administrative reform.

REFERENCES

Mao Zedong. n.d. *Selected Works of Mao Zedong*, vol. III, p. 83.

——. 1992. *Public Administration and Municipal Administration in Singapore.* Guangzhou: Zhongshan University Press.

——. 1991. ed. *Public Administration.* Guangzhou: Zhongshan University Press.

——. 1991. *Public Administration in Hong Kong.* Beijing: Guangming Daily Press.

——. 1988. *New Approaches to Public Administration.* Hubei: n.p.

Xia Shuzhang, ed. 1990. *Municipal Administration.* Beijing: Higher Educational Press.

——. ed. 1990. *Municipal Administration in China.* Beijing: Knowledge Press.

——. 1987. *Administration, Psychology, and Medicine.* Beijing: Law Press.

——. 1987. *Modern Administration and "Three Kingdoms" Story.* Changsha: Hunan Science and Technology Press.

——. 1986. *Eight Lectures on Municipal Administration.* Taiyuan: Shanxi Publishing House.

——. 1986. *New Approaches in Public Administration.* Beijing: Political Science and Law University Press.

——. 1985. *Lectures on Administration in Higher Education.* Taiyuan: Shanxi Publishing House.

——. 1985. *Personnel Administration.* Beijing: People's Publishing House.

——. 1985. *Public Administration.* Taiyuan: Shanxi Publishing House.

——. 1984. *Administration, Ethics, and Law.* Beijing: Law Press.

CHAPTER 10

A Frequent Visitor's Perspective

King W. Chow

King W. Chow discusses a contemporary perspective of public administration and theory-building in the People's Republic of China. He has been a frequent traveler and has exhaustively examined the status of public administration. His is a uniquely focused perspective based on data assembled both before and after the events of Tiananman Square on June 4, 1989. He acknowledges that, unfortunately, many contemporary Chinese scholars of public administration tend to provide descriptive studies rather than address the critical concerns of theory-building. He notes that even American public administration has also been criticized for being insufficiently rigorous. As he notes, American scholars ''have yet to generate elegant theories characterized by simplicity, relevance, and predictive power.''

Since the Chinese cadres have not seen the benefit of productive or useful theory-building, they do not rely on public administrators as a guide to their performance. These misgivings have tended to make the task of public administration research even more difficult, since researchers face obstacles in gaining access to information. This trend has been heightened by greater reserve and caution since the June 4 crackdown.

Chow comments that research methodology is predominantly qualitative rather than quantitative, and he laments the limited training that Chinese scholars have received. Chow also reports that the government has steadily been imposing greater controls on the academics by emphasizing unquestioning loyalty to the regime. This insecurity is certainly not conducive to positive research activities. He suggests that the scholars may tend to focus on those inquiries that are unlikely to stir official displeasure. He concludes by stressing the importance of better training for researchers and more interchange with Western scholars. Chow has

accomplished a great deal in sharing appropriate and responsive Western
methods with his many Chinese colleagues.

Having a genuine interest in Chinese politics and administration, I have visited
China frequently in the past fifteen years. Since 1983, I have interviewed
approximately 200 state cadres, academics, and residents in Beijing, Chengdu.
Dailin, Guangzhou, Jinlin, Tianjin, and Xian to collect information about
administrative problems and the development of Chinese public administration
(as a field of study). As a result, I am somewhat more familiar than other China
watchers with the state of Chinese public administration (PA). Since a detailed
description of the development of the field, as well as issues and prospects, is
already in print (Chow 1991; see also Zhang 1986, chap. 3), I will focus only
on the critical issue of theory building; the analysis will be based mainly on data
collected after a military crackdown in Beijing on June 4, 1989. The purpose is
to generate a basis for PA scholars, inside and outside China, to develop a better
understanding of the problems of theory-building and to search for effective
measures for coping with those problems.

THE ISSUE OF THEORY-BUILDING

As Zhang (1986, chap. 3) has indicated, the rapid development of PA in China
is impressive. By the end of 1982, only one journalistic article on public
administration (Xia 1982) had been published, and few scholars considered the
field their specialty. By mid-1987, however, there were more than 100 institutes
offering PA courses; eighty-plus PA textbooks were in print; close to ten academic
journals devoted to the advancement of the art and science of public administration
were in circulation; and more than 1,000 scholars claimed to have an expertise
or a genuine interest in PA.

Although the Chinese PA scholars are generally pleased with the rapid
development of PA in the past few years, they do recognize that the efforts expended
are merely for the promotion of the discipline in China. As one Chinese PA scholar
commented, "Public Administration has never had a root in China, and a massive
campaign is needed to promote and legitimize the study; now, more people,
particularly government officials and academicians, are aware of the significance
of the discipline; PA is likely to be a well established field of study in the coming
decade" (interview with a PA professor in Tianjin on August 9, 1987).

Nevertheless, whether Chinese PA can become a full-fledged discipline depends
very much on how well scholars manage to establish PA theories, a difficult task
that committed researchers have to perform (Denhardt 1990). A review of major
PA literature (see, for example, Tang 1986; D. Wang 1986; H. Wang 1986; Xia
1985; Ying 1985, 1986; Yue 1986; Zhang 1986), unfortunately, indicates that
most contemporary Chinese PA scholars are, from the perspective of behavioralists,
"unconscious thinkers." Their works are merely descriptive studies, analyses of
administrative issues, or "how-to-do-it" prescriptions of management processes.

They are, at best, interpretative research aimed at the development of a better understanding of administrative phenomena in China. Interpretative research has its place in theory-building (White 1986a): description and interpretation are essential to developing a somewhat complete understanding of certain relationships in this world characterized by complexity and uncertainty. But interpretative research must be kept in its place; it should result in a basis for empirical research leading to the establishment of theoretical prepositions. Otherwise, scholars will remain in the state of "getting ready to get ready" (Sigelman 1976, 623), and theories will never be constructed.

Chinese PA scholars and practitioners are also aware of the problem. As one scholar noted: "The primary problem of the development of PA at this point of time is theory-building. More people are now accepting PA as a field of study. Nevertheless, if PA is to become a legitimate discipline, it must have a set of theories applicable to explaining and predicting administrative phenomena in socialist China. Current publications, however, lack these elements" (interview with a PA researcher of the Academy of Social Sciences of China in Beijing on August 11, 1987). Another scholar commented, "It will be mistaken to consider the study of problems in the workplace an academic discipline; without a preconceived mission—generating systematic knowledge about administrative process—we [PA scholars] are nothing but practitioners or journalists interested in public administrative issues" (interview with a PA professor in Beijing on August 15, 1987).

One practitioner, who participated in the organizing work for an association of public administration at the provincial level, stated, "Scholars have been working hard to establish the discipline and we practitioners do support their struggle; however, we cannot pretend that they [scholars] have given us what we desperately need—theories that guide our decision-making and problem-solving" (interview with a bureau-grade cadre in Guangzhou on April 7, 1988). Another practitioner with a similar background as Xian gave a similar criticism (interview with a bureau-grade cadre on July 8, 1990).

I have heard nothing good about the progress of theory-building in the past few years. Based on information collected in two field trips in July and August 1990, I believe that theory-building remains a very critical issue. This, however, does not imply the impossibility of the coming of age of Chinese PA; it merely reflects that Chinese PA scholars are following the steps of their counterparts in the United States.

The Issue of Theory-building in the United States

Recent research has shown that theory-building within the field of American PA is also problematic. Based on an analysis of 142 dissertation abstracts published in *Dissertation Abstracts International*, McCurdy and Cleary (1984) find that most doctoral dissertations published in 1981–82 dealt with insignificant research problems and that the reliability of many of the findings presented was questionable.

A replication of McCurdy and Cleary's research (with a sample of 305 dissertation abstracts published in 1980 and 1981) by White (1986b) also suggests that few dissertations presented rigorous logical analysis and persuasive argument. The author noted, "Roughly half of the research does not conform to the standards of mainstream social science and therefore does not have the potential to contribute to the growth of knowledge in public administration" (229).

A more alarming complaint has been filed by Perry and Kraemer (1986; see also Perry and Kraemer [1990] for a similar critique). Their review of the contents and methodology of articles published in *Public Administration Review* (*PAR*) between 1975 and 1984 reveals that even research reports published in *PAR*, a prominent mainstream journal, could be considered unsatisfactory.

First, public administration research is primarily "applied" rather than "basic." Nearly three-fourths of the articles dealt with either problem delineation or variable identification; less than one-fourth dealt with theoretical relationships among variables. Moreover, the research lacks detachment from immediate and instrumental concerns. Most of the articles reporting on empirical research were of either the case study or cross-sectional survey variety; few articles involved field experiments, structural equations, or longitudinal studies. Finally, the underlying purposes of doing research tend to be problem oriented, which limits development and testing of empirical theory. (221)

Whereas public administration research has been predominantly applied, as Perry and Kraemer (1986) have rightly pointed out, there is no guarantee that those findings are relevant to problem solving in the workplace. Indeed, I have personally heard (American, Chinese, and Hong Kong) practitioners' comments criticizing or doubting the value, applicability, and transferability of public administration theories: "those theories are merely commonsense knowledge"; "those theories are so abstract that no one, including theorists themselves, can tell when and under what conditions should they be applied"; "public administration theories are ivory tower inventions and when applied in the workplace, they are more a burden than panacea to our problems."

In light of the criticisms from both researchers and practitioners, the problems of scholarship and theory-building in the field of American PA must be acknowledged. Admittedly, scholars have yet to generate elegant theories characterized by simplicity, relevance, and predictive power; too often they cannot establish empirically verified propositions to accurately describe the public administrative reality and plausibly explain the occurrence of events.

The Quest for Theories in China

American scholars and practitioners are displeased with the poverty of theories; their counterparts in China are equally displeased. One senior official at the State Council recently complained (July 5, 1990, Beijing), "I myself was a professor of public administration and did not find the theoretical elements in the current literature satisfactory; as of today, I am still displeased for too many of the books and articles give only description and too little works have been done to identify causal relationships.'' One key administrator at the National School of Administration of China commented (July 6, 1990, Beijing):

We have much problems in identifying relevant and useful materials for our teaching programs because current research reports present mainly findings that are available also in journalistic outlets; there are basically nothing theoretical and nothing new. Moreover, theories reported in Western literatures cannot be applied in Socialist China without modification. Yet, no scholars are making that kind of effort! Seemingly, unless Chinese PA scholars are more concerned with theoretical analysis, we would never have theories taught at our School.

Practitioners and academicians at the provincial level are also unhappy with the state of the art. One senior official in charge of a bureau in a province stated (July 11, 1990, Xian): ''I am involved in public affairs, as well as the administration work of our provincial association of public administration. I can tell you that cadres do not find those so-called theories useful, or even relevant, to their problem-solving, and that scholars themselves are hardly in the position to claim that they have any theories to offer to practitioners.'' One teacher at a provincial institute of administration also complained (July 13, 1990, Chengdu), ''We are surely embarrassed by the lack of PA theories when students ask which book or journal has presented theories that they can study and then apply in the workplace.''

CAUSES OF THE UNDERDEVELOPMENT OF THEORIES

I interacted with at least thirty PA scholars in the past six years, and none of them felt comfortable to claim possession of theories; some even admitted that they did not know what constituted a theory. Seemingly, something must be done if the quest for theories is to be fruitful. The first step is to identify the major causes of the problem.

What Has Been Said

As reported elsewhere (Chow 1991), there are three major causes of underdevelopment of theories in China in the past years. First, Chinese scholars have always had difficulties in gaining access to information from government officials. This is so mainly because cadres have been receptive to the secrecy rule. The rule was legitimized on the basis of the need to protect the interest of the state. Since 1949, the regime has repeatedly claimed the existence of possible threats from the Kuomintang in Taiwan and from the United States; these claims have justified the alleged imperative for the leadership to conceal information about policy adoption and personnel decisions in the past four decades. Since information is a source of power, the application of the rule in effect reduces the power and autonomy of most cadres. Consequently, they are not in the position to challenge decisions made at the top. The use of the secrecy rule thus serves to facilitate the regime's control of the bureaucracy. A side effect has been that since cadres have internalized the norm of secrecy, they feel comfortable concealing information from the public generally and the academicians in particular.

Whereas the State Council has recently instructed state organs to release unclassified information to researchers when requested, administrative secrecy remains the norm. Access to information has become impossible for almost all researchers since the June 4 military crackdown. The current leadership has attempted to tighten political control, and thus cadres are feeling very insecure and are even more reluctant to cooperate with academicians. PA scholars thus find empirical research to be either infeasible or frustrating. These perceptions and feelings are understandable. I myself have found that even many of my former respondents who were rather frank and outspoken became cautious and diplomatic when I interviewed them after the military crackdown. I could collect from them only information that was available also from official news reports and publications.

Second, complete research methodology has yet to be developed. Chinese scholars have been employing mainly qualitative methods, such as historical analysis, case study, content analysis, and unstructured interviewing, which are less rigorous as compared with quantitative methods in terms of standardization, precision, and data manipulation, which facilitate the building of "elegant" theories. And third, resolution of the problem of trained incapacity is awaiting. Most Chinese PA scholars are hardly capable of conducting rigorous empirical research and are not committed to theory-building because they have received very little or no training in positive research.

The problems of underdevelopment of methodology and trained incapacity are inevitable due to the weak basis of the field. After the Chinese Communist Party (CCP) came into power in 1949, major universities still offered public administration courses. In 1952, however, Mao Zedong and his followers considered administrative theories based on capitalist values to be irrelevant to their socialist pursuits. They thus instructed universities to eliminate PA courses. PA as a field of study vanished between 1952 and 1982, and scholars shifted their teaching and research focus from public administrative theories to other areas, such as political economy, Marxist-Leninism, and history.

Since the late 1970s, the shift of policy focus from class struggle to economic development has resulted in a demand for rational administration. Between December 1983 and January 1984, Professor Xia Shuzhang, who had published a journalistic article on January 29, 1982, in *Renmin Ribao (People's Daily)*—the official newspaper of the CCP—in which he called for a systematic study of administration, offered a two-month program on public administration for university teachers interested in the subject matter. Close to forty scholars attended the training program held in Shanghai. Subsequent developments indicated the significance and success of Xia's program: program participants openly advocated the establishment of PA; various cadre-training colleges and major universities began to offer PA courses; some cadre-training colleges offered PA as a major; and many provinces established PA associations.

Nevertheless, the leading PA scholars, particularly those who had attended the Shanghai program, are now responsible for training young PA scholars and have not received training in positive research and methodology. They have pursued research in such areas as political philosophy and history. Thus, they are hardly in a position to offer rigorous training in social scientific investigation to the second and third generation of PA scholars.

My interactions with Chinese PA scholars, old and young, have reflected that the scholars are primarily concerned with description or problem delineation. They often apply such concepts as political neutrality and administrative competence without careful elaboration; they rarely try to operationalize constructs before analyzing causal relationships; they generally omit hypothesis testing and treat speculations as valid theoretical propositions; some young scholars cannot even identify the differences between inductive and deductive reasoning. Most important, many PA teachers, particularly those in cadre-training institutes at the provincial level, are not familiar with the nature and problems of social scientific investigation, and quite a few of them cannot tell what exactly as theory is. Obviously, if the masters are not well trained, neither will be their students; future scholars will also be trapped in this vicious cycle.

Emerging Problems since the Crackdown

The problem mentioned above is amenable to solutions (to be discussed). But two new problems have emerged since the June 4 military crackdown, problems that are much more difficult to tackle: tightened political control and reification. Regarding the former, I have learned from respondents that the current leadership has introduced a variety of measures to keep the bureaucracy and the academic community under tight control: reregistration of CCP membership, a measure to give party leadership an opportunity to screen out members with questionable loyalty; re-empowerment of party secretariats, a measure to strip the power of chief executive officers of state organs, enterprises, and other state-supported organizations, including universities and cadre-training institutes; and re-empowerment of party members, encouraging them to file reports about questionable loyalty of nonparty members.

Due to those control measures, PA scholars feel extremely insecure and dare not conduct research on issues that relate to the monopoly of powers by the party. Thus, whereas separation of the party from the state was a hot topic in 1988, few scholars now would make comments about it (or when they do, they merely repeat the official policy line) because they might be accused of supporting Zhao Ziyang, the former party secretary general. Whereas administrative ethics was becoming an attractive issue in the late 1980s, few would try to address the issue now because they are afraid that some people might criticize them for using administrative ethics as a weapon to discredit party leadership (this is, in a sense, true because many unethical behaviors in the bureaucracy stem from the monopoly of powers by the party).

Given the current political constraints, many PA scholars feel frustrated and lack the motivation to conduct research. One young PA scholar in Beijing (who may be considered a rising star) said, "I can hardly forget what had happened in last June [1989] and I can also feel all those political pressures; why should I work hard when the leadership does not appreciate my research work and would probably punish me for doing it?" (interview conducted in July 1990; interview information withheld to protect the informant).

Another young researcher in Sichuan complained, "I received my graduate training in Journalism and had chosen to become a PA scholar, but it was a serious mistake; right now, I can't teach what I like—politics and administration dichotomy—and our Party secretariat has instructed us to avoid research issues that reflect the defects and flaws of Marxist-Leninist state." "How can we do that," she continued, "when administrative problems are either directly or indirectly caused by the political structure!" (interview conducted in July 1990; interview information withheld to protect the informant). She said that she had to give up PA research and shift her focus to the study of "public relations"!

If there is a will, there is a way. Chinese PA scholars may still pursue research that is of theoretical and practical significance. Yet, due to reification—treating the reality as static and beyond one's control—many of them have given up. Based on my interviews conducted in 1989–90, I believe that almost all PA researchers (except those who are well connected with high-level cadres) feel that they can do very little to change the present political reality and that their research findings cannot serve as a basis for reconstructing the reality. Most of them believe that they need to work on research problems that are fundamental: how power should be redistributed within the polity; how the party should be kept accountable; how good-old-boy networks should be broken down. Otherwise, the research findings are insignificant and cannot form a basis for guiding political and administrative reforms. Yet, since all these research problems are related to the issues of the desirability of Marxism-Leninism and the monopoly of power by the present leadership (and its followers), PA researchers cannot proceed. Thus, they do not believe that they can pursue meaningful research or that their research findings can become a basis for the making of rational reform policies. (Some young scholars, who want to leave the country, are still working hard because they want to establish their publication record so as to secure overseas financial support for graduate studies.) They feel vulnerable, and they give up; like other ordinary citizens, they are now primarily concerned with how to make a better living, rather than how to advance PA knowledge.

WHAT IS TO BE DONE?

Chinese PA scholars generally recognize that the quest for theories is essential to the coming of age of Chinese PA and that the transfer of PA theories from

Western democracies is hardly a viable solution. Yet, they also feel that their hands are tied; they find it difficult to cope with the problems of limited access to information, underdevelopment of methodology, trained incapacity, tightened political control, and reification.

Since I spent almost ten years in Texas, I have subscribed myself to the frontier spirit, believing in the motto "If there is a will, there is a way." Thus, I believe that the five problems are amenable to solutions. Specifically, I think that three remedial actions can be taken: training in theory building, objectification, and the repoliticization of PA.

Train the Researchers

In view of the vicious cycle aforementioned, the insufficient training in theory-building and research methodology, is likely to remain a serious problem. Nevertheless, this does not imply that theory-building in China is a mission impossible. My interactions with young Chinese PA scholars in the past years have revealed that most young scholars are very intelligent and trainable. For instance, after I gave a seminar in July 1990 to graduate students and teachers at Peking University on the state of the art of American PA research, many of them were quick in picking up my criticisms and could apply those criticisms in the Chinese administration context.

Chinese PA scholars are trainable, but PA scholars in Western democracies should help to provide rigorous training in theory-building to their counterparts in China, if they subscribe to the code of ethics—"encourage the professional development of our associates and those seeking to enter the field of public administration" (American Society for Public Administration). Some American scholars have already traveled to China to give lectures. One Canadian university even established a joint master's program in public administration with the People's University of China. Yet, with the exception of the cases of Stuart S. Nagel and Peter deLeon (see below), those efforts have contributed relatively little to the systematic advancement of PA knowledge in China. The simple reason is that lectures on current research findings about public administrative events in Western democracies can hardly become usable knowledge in China. Borrowed management tools and techniques can never be effectively applied unless various constraints and ecological impacts on policy-making and administration in socialist China have been comprehensively understood. This means that somehow there must be scholars pursuing theoretical analysis of the causes and effects of Chinese policy-making and administration before anything else. Obviously, they should be Chinese PA scholars themselves. This also underscores that theory-building training, rather than importation of "theories," is paramount and that Western scholars must help their counterparts who are poorly trained.

In this light, two things need to be done. First, the importation of such rigorous research techniques as experiments, formal modeling, and surveys should be arranged. And second, Chinese PA scholars should receive from Western scholars the training to master a strict application of normative methodology or logical procedures, including formulating research problems, constructing theories, deriving hypotheses, and operationalizing concepts.

The assistance should be fruitful. For example, after Stuart S. Nagel (University of Illinois) gave a series of lectures on the policy studies method in Guangzhou and Beijing (May 1989), many Chinese PA researchers, as well as practitioners became more self-conscious of the significance of the policy studies method. After Peter deLeon (University of Colorado) gave a series of lectures on the policy process model in Guangzhou and Beijing (May 1990), many Chinese PA researchers became more aware of the usefulness of theoretical frameworks.

I represent another example, in that after I gave a lecture to graduate students and young teachers of the Institute of Administrative Sciences at the People's University of China on theoretical analysis and typology of causation, some could then classify current Chinese PA literature, and others could come up with plausible research problems. One young teacher even came to me after the lecture to discuss how he could conduct research on the exploration of necessary conditions. Citing my lecture on Straussman and Rosenberg's (1984) analysis of productivity improvement efforts (PIE), he asked if we can—based on Straussman and Rosenberg's proposition that PIE is possible only if "we can make the attainment of their personal goals (income, prestige, etc.) contingent on the achievement of the politically determined objective"(281)—argue that individual benefits for the civil servant are a necessary condition for productivity gains in the public sector. Can we? That is exactly the argument presented by Straussman and Rosenberg, two leading PA professors!

Objectification and Repoliticization of PA

Outside assistance may help to break the vicious cycle of inadequate training, but more important, Chinese PA scholars must help themselves. As mentioned in the preceding section, most of them believe that they need to work on "important" research problems that are directly related to the issues of the desirability of Marxism—Leninism and the monopoly of power by the present leadership (and its followers). Thus, in light of the current political constraints, they feel frustrated. For example, some PA scholars have been pursuing research on the problems of establishing a merit-based civil service system. One major issue concerns selection of recruitment and promotion criteria. To the political leaders, unquestionable loyalty is as important as ability and administrative performance; to PA scholars, loyalty should not be a meritorious criterion. Since their research would inevitably reflect their policy position, which is in conflict with that of the leaders, leaders are thus hardly receptive to their findings, and some even take actions to stop them from conducting research. One teacher in a provincial training institute told me that he and his colleagues were instructed by the party leaders that they should not advocate ideas that were in conflict with those of the leaders. In light of those political constraints and pressure, many PA scholars perceive the impossibility of research.

This, however, is a misperception, and it can be changed if they receive advice and support from outsiders. For example, when I visited Beijing in August 1990, I had numerous opportunities to interact with young scholars, and my sharing of insights was fruitful. Specifically, I presented to them two arguments. First, although modification of the current political reality, which is socially constructed, is always possible, the change may be progressive or retrogressive. To ensure progression, scholars should strive to establish empirically verified propositions about the causes of political and administrative phenomena in China so that both political leaders and the general public can have a basis for making rational decisions in the sociopolitical development process. This means that the relationship between theory-building and political constraints is interactional: scholars must take actions to establish theories under the current political constraints in order to modify those constraints. This also means that scholars must strive to objectify a new reality, one characterized by logic, empiricism, and objectivity, so that other people can follow their lead.

And second, although public administration is inevitably an extension of the political process and although public administration is definitely a politicized activity, the level of politicization varies, depending on the unique nature and characteristics of a particular administrative activity. Thus, it is incorrect to assume that all PA research problems are equally politicized.

In light of my advice, many PA scholars have begun to appreciate that (1) reification is permanent only if they do not try to objectify a new reality; (2) a general theory of public administration in socialist China is essential to the reconstruction of the current political reality; (3) such a theory can hardly be established when most of the stones are left unturned; and (4) the immediate action to take is to strive to establish propositions about the causes of administrative phenomena that are relatively ''nonpolitical.'' Most important, they now realize that the depoliticization of PA—conducting research in a politics-free context—neither is possible nor is the only alternative for systematically advancing PA knowledge and that they may work on even politically significant problems if they are politically skillful.

Some inspired young scholars are now determined to cope with reification and are trying to repoliticize PA, that is, to employ political strategies and tactics in their academic pursuit. These scholars aim to analyze some ''seemingly'' neutral research problems and to present the findings without stressing their political implications. For example, when I visited Xian (July 1990), I held a seminar on clinical experiment and its potential contributions to theory-building. Seminar participants were very receptive and were able to identify quite a few interesting research problems that can be effectively accommodated by clinical experiment. It was then suggested by one PA teacher that although political democracy and participation are desirable, little is known about the necessary condition for ''effective'' participation in decision making in China. After I introduced the participants to the groupthink theory (Janis 1972; Whyte 1989), the obedience-to-authority proposition (Milgram 1974), and the conformity theory (Penrod 1983), the teacher and other participants were able to identify the behavioral tendency to reject blind submission to authority as a possible necessary condition for egalitarian participation and to propose viable experimental designs for confirming the causal relationship. Most important, they also decided to present their research problem in such a way that, notwithstanding its political implications, the current leadership would not find the research a challenge to its governance. The researchers would claim that the research is merely about how democratic participation in the administrative decision-making process can be effected so as to promote administrative efficiency and effectiveness, rather than about the inapplicability of the Marxist-Leninist type of organizational arrangement and practices for governance.

Consider another example. I reported to participants of a seminar held in Chengdu (July 1990) the following. First, research findings presented in the 1970s suggest that men are better leaders than women, that men and women may differ in personality characteristics that affect leadership style and effectiveness, and that men and women do differ in leadership behaviors and effectiveness. Second, Dobbins and Platz (1986) conducted a meta-analysis of seventeen studies examining sex differences in leadership and found that overall, men and women as leaders exhibit equal amounts of initiating structure and consideration and have equally satisfied subordinates. Moreover, I pointed out that the issue of sex differences in leadership has important implications not only for administrators but also for those concerned with building an egalitarian society.

In light of my report, some participants, particularly the female teachers, showed much interest in conducting similar research in the Chinese bureaucracy in order to address the following questions: Are there any sex differences in leadership? If so, what are the causes and effects of the differences? What are the major administrative and political implications? They also planned to present an apolitical justification of their research problem: it is important to identify the causes and effects of sex differences in leadership so that administrative efficiency and effectiveness can be enhanced.

There are other examples. Some scholars have decided to conduct research on the relationship between the urge to achieve (McCelland 1978) and job performance (both administrative and political) so as to discredit the leadership's argument that political loyalty should be the prime criterion for staffing decision making. Others, based on my report about Agor's (1984, 1985a, and 1985b) findings, plan to study the relationship between brain-skill management and the making of politically and technically feasible administrative decisions so as to come up with a micro-level theory for the rationalization of decision making without directly challenging the practice of monopoly of power by the party. Still other scholars are now planning on translating Downs's *Inside Bureaucracy* (1967) and eventually testing the hypotheses presented in that classic book for the purpose of establishing propositions that defy the current hierarchical structure of the bureaucracy in particular and of the polity in general.

In addition to the examples given above, some scholars have realized that the repoliticization of PA is also one effective way to cope with the problem of limited access to information. In the past, they merely tried to ask for information from bureaucrats, who were invariably suspicious and reluctant to cooperate. With the repoliticization of PA as the guiding principle, many now recognize that they should try to be politically skillful in data collection. Some have stated that they will try to develop better personal ties with leading cadres so that, after mutual trust has been established, cadres will be willing to help them in gaining information. Others plan to present their research projects to cadres in such a way that the findings will be of direct benefit to cadres and, thus, cadres will be more cooperative. For instance, based on my report about the values of mentorship (Henderson 1985; Schott 1986), one researcher plans to examine how mentorship is related to the bureaucratic tendency to cultivate personal ties, a major cause of many administrative problems (Chow 1988). Yet, he plans to inform cadres that the research is about the relationship between mentorship and effective leadership, which will generate findings that could promote executive development and administrative effectiveness.

In sum, my interactions with Chinese PA scholars reflect that they are trainable and are receptive to advice from outsiders. Seemingly, organized efforts by scholars in Western democracies may help to resolve the critical problems of PA theory-building in China.

CONCLUSION

Since the present leaders, including those who participated in the June 4 military crackdown, are pushing for rapid economic development, PA, generally considered an applied science, is likely to become an increasingly important field of study. Nevertheless, in light of the problems of limited access to information, underdevelopment of methodology, trained incapacity, tightened political control, and reification, Chinese PA scholars find theory-building difficult. In view of the state of the art of theory-building in Western democracies, it is naive to assume that all those obstacles to theory-building in China can be immediately and completely removed. Nevertheless, the analysis presented here reveals that the problems are amenable to solutions and that three remedial measures—training, objectification, and repoliticization of PA—may facilitate the pursuit of theory-building.

Possibly effective measures have been identified. The issues now are whether the Chinese scholars will undertake those recommended remedial actions and whether their counterparts in Western democracies will try to help.

REFERENCES

Agor, Weston H. 1985a. "Managing Brain Skills to Increase Productivity." *Public Administration Review* 45 (6):864–68.

——. 1985b. "Intuition: A Brain Skill Top Executives Use to Increase Productivity." *Public Productivity Review* 9 (4):357–72.

—— . 1984. "Using Brain Skill Assessments to Increase Productivity in Development Administration." *International Journal of Public Administration* 6 (4):471–479.

Chow, King W. 1991. "Chinese Public Administration as a Discipline: Development, Issues, and Prospects." In Ali Farazmand, ed., *Handbook of Comparative and Development Administration*. New York: Marcel Dekker.

—— . 1988. "The Management of Chinese Cadre Resources: The Politics of Performance Appraisal (1949–1984)." *International Review of Administrative Sciences* 54 (3):359–78.

Denhardt, Robert B. 1990. "Public Administration: The State of the Discipline." In Naomi B. Lynn and Aaron Wildavsky, eds., *Public Administration: The State of the Discipline*. Chatham, N.J.: Chatham House Publishers.

Dobbins, Gregory H., and Stephanie J. Platz. 1986. "Sex Differences in Leadership: How Real Are They?" *Academy of Management Review* 11 (1):118–27.

Downs, Anthony. 1967. *Inside Bureaucracy*. Boston: Little, Brown, and Co.

Henderson, Dee W. 1985. "Enlightened Mentoring: A Characteristic of Public Management Professionalism." *Public Administration Review* 45 (6):857–63.

Inglehart, Ronald. 1988. "The Renaissance of Political Culture." *American Political Science Review* 82 (4):1203–30.

Janis, Irving L. 1972. *Groupthink*. 2d ed. Boston: Houghton Mifflin Co.

McCelland, David. 1978. "That Urge to Achieve." In Walter E. Natemeyer, ed., *Classics of Organizational Behavior*. Oak Park, Ill: Moore Publishing Co.

McCurdy, Howard E., and Robert E. Cleary. 1984. "Why Can't We Resolve the Research Issue in Public Administration?" *Public Administration Review* 44 (1):49–55.

Milgram, Stanley. 1974. *Obedience to Authority: An Experimental View*. New York: Harper and Row.

Penrod, Steven. 1983. *Social Psychology*. Englewood Cliffs, N.J.: Prentice-Hall.

Perry, James L., and Kenneth L. Kraemer. 1990. "Research Methodology in Public Administration: Issues and Patterns." In Naomi B. Lynn and Aaron Wildavsky, eds., *Public Administration: The State of the Discipline*. Chatham, N.J.: Chatham House Publishers.

—— . 1986. "Research Methodology in the *Public Administration Review*." *Public Administration Review* 46 (3):215–26.

Schott, Richard L. 1986. "The Psychological Development of Adults: Implications for Public Administration." *Public Administration Review* 46 (6):657–67.

Sigelman, Lee. 1976. "In Search of Comparative Administration." *Public Administration Review* 2 (36):621–25.

Straussman, Jeffrey, and A. Rosenberg. 1984. "Maximization, Markets, and the Measurement of Productivity in the Public Sector." In Barry Bozeman and Jeffrey Straussman, eds., *New Directions in Public Administration*. Monterey, Calif.: Brooks/Cole Publishing Co.

Tang, D. W. 1986. *Xian Dai Xing Zheng Guan Li Xue*. (*Contemporary Public Administration*). Chang Sha: Ji She Chu Ban She.

Wang, D. Y. 1986. *Xing Zheng Guan Li Xue (Public Administration)*. Gui Zhou: Gui Zhou Renmin Chu Ban She.

Wang, H. Y. 1986. *Xing Zheng Guan Li Xue Jiang Zuo (Lectures on Public Administration)*. Chang Chen: Ji Lin Renmin Chu Ban Sha.

White, Jay D. 1986a. "On the Growth of Knowledge in Public Administration." *Public Administration Review* 46 (1):15–24.

———. 1986b. "Dissertations and Publications in Public Administration." *Public Administration Review* 46 (3):227–34.

Whyte, Glen. 1989. "Groupthink Reconsidered." *Academy of Management Review* 14 (1):40–57.

Xia Shuzhang, ed. 1985. *Xing Zheng Guan Li Xue (Public Administration)*. Tai Yuan: Shan Xi Ren Min Chu Ban She.

———. 1982. *Renmin Ribao*, January 29.

Ying, S. N. 1986. *Xing Zheng Fa Xue Zong Lun (Introduction to Public Administrative Law)*. Beijing: Gong Rem Chu Ban She.

———. 1985. *Xing Zheng Guen Li Xue (Public Administration)*. Beijing: Beijing Shi Fan Da Xiu Chu Ban She.

Yue, Z. R. 1986. *Zong Guo Xing Zheng Guan Li Xue (Chinese Public Administration)*. Limen: Li Men Gu Ren Min Chu Ban She.

Zhang, Y. F., ed. 1986. *Ren Shi Guan Li Xue (Personnel Administration)*. Chang Sha: Hu Nan Ke Xue Ji Shu Chu Ban She.

Name Index

Subject Index

About the Editors and Contributors

MIRIAM K. MILLS was a professor of management at the New Jersey Institute of Technology in Newark, New Jersey before her death in 1992. She had her doctorate in public administration from New York University. Dr. Mills wrote extensively on labor relations, health policy, and dispute resolution. Her most recent books include *Dispute Resolution in the Public Sector* (1990) and *Conflict Resolution and Public Policy* (Greenwood, 1990). She coauthored or coedited several books, including *Biomedical Technology and Public Policy* (Greenwood, 1989); *Evaluation Analysis with Microcomputers* (1988); and *Multi-Criteria Methods and Dispute Resolution* (Greenwood, 1990).

STUART S. NAGEL is a professor of political science at the University of Illinois. He is the secretary-treasurer and publications coordinator for the Policy Studies Organization. He is the author or editor of such relevant books as *Policy Studies: Integration and Evaluation* (Praeger, 1988); *Global Policy Studies: International Interaction toward Improving Public Policy* (1990); and *Developing Nations and Super-Optimum Policy Analysis* (1991). He has conducted training workshops on systematic policy analysis, decision-aiding software, and super-optimum solutions in such places as the People's Republic of China, Hong Kong, the Philippines, Morocco, Kenya, Zambia, Panama, Argentina, Brazil, Yugoslavia, Germany, France, Switzerland, Italy, South Africa, Israel, and the United States.

HON S. CHAN is a lecturer in the Department of Public and Social Administration at the City Polytechnic of Hong Kong.

K. C. CHEUNG is a senior lecturer in the Department of Management Studies at Hong Kong Polytechnic in Kowloon.

KING W. CHOW, formerly assistant professor of political science at Texas Tech University, now teaches at the University of Hong Kong. He has published many articles on public administration in China in such journals as *Asian Profile, International Journal of Public Administration, International Review of Administrative Sciences, Issues, and Studies,* and *Public Budgeting and Financial Management.*

THOMAS R. DYE is McKenzie Professor of Government and director of Policy Sciences at Florida State University. He is the author of numerous books on public policy and policy analysis.

PETER NAN-SHONG LEE is the chairman of the Department of Government and Public Administration at the Chinese University of Hong Kong. His most recent publications include *Industrial Management and Economic Reform in China, 1949-1984* (1988).

JACK M. K. LO is a lecturer in the Department of Management Studies at Hong Kong Polytechnic in Kowloon.

SUN GUANGDE is a professor at the People's University of China Institute of Labour and Personnel and a professor at Beijing Medical University. She is a trustee of the Labour Society of China and a consultant for the Chinese Society of Health Economics. Among her recent writings are *Health Economics* and *Labour Economics.* Professor Sun is a chief editor of *Social Insurance and Staff Welfare.*

TANG DAIWANG is dean of the Administration Department at the Institute of Administration in Guangdong Province. He is a member of the Council of the General National Society for Administrative Research and the Center of Social Education Research and is on the Ministry of Civil Administration in the People's Republic of China.

XIA SHUZHANG is vice-chairman of the University Board of Zhongshan University in Guangzhou. He is vice-president of the Chinese Political Science Association, the Chinese Public Administration Association, and the Chinese People's Institute of Foreign Affairs. He is an adviser to the China Research Society of Urban Sciences and Administrative Law. He is the author of numerous books and articles on public administration, including *Public Administration* (1985), *Personnel Administration* (1985), *New Approaches in Public Administration* (1986), and *Lectures on Administration in Higher Education* (1985).

ZHAO BAOXU is with the Department of International Politics at Beijing University. He is the director of the Research Center for Social Development of Contemporary China and is on the Executive Council of the Chinese Association of Political Science. Professor Zhao is also president of the Beijing Association for Political Science.

Policy Studies Organization publications issued with Greenwood Press/Quorum Books

Health Insurance and Public Policy: Risk, Allocation, and Equity
Miriam K. Mills and Robert H. Blank, editors

Public Authorities and Public Policy: The Business of Government
Jerry Mitchell, editor

Technology and U.S. Competitiveness: An Institutional Focus
W. Henry Lambright and Dianne Rahm, editors

Using Theory to Improve Program and Policy Evaluations
Huey-tysh Chen and Peter H. Rossi, editors

Comparative Judicial Review and Public Policy
Donald W. Jackson and C. Neal Tate, editors

Moving the Earth: Cooperative Federalism and Implementation of the Surface Mining Act
Uday Desai, editor

Professional Developments in Policy Studies
Stuart Nagel

International Agricultural Trade and Market Development in the 1990s
John W. Helmuth and Don F. Hadwiger, editors

Comparative Studies of Local Economic Development: Problems in Policy Implementation
Peter B. Meyer, editor

Ownership, Control, and the Future of Housing Policy
R. Allen Hays, editor

Public Administration in China
Miriam K. Mills and Stuart S. Nagel, editors